Drush User's Guide

A practical guide to Drush, Drupal's command line interface, helping you work with your Drupal sites more effectively

Juan Pablo Novillo Requena

BIRMINGHAM - MUMBAI

Drush User's Guide

First published: April 2012

Production Reference: 1020412

Published by Packt Publishing Ltd.
Livery Place
35 Livery Street
Birmingham B3 2PB, UK..

ISBN 978-1-84951-798-0

www.packtpub.com

Cover Image by Asher Wishkerman (a.wishkerman@mpic.de)

Credits

Author
  Juan Pablo Novillo Requena

Reviewer
  Greg Anderson

  Jonathan Araña Cruz

Acquisition Editor
  Joanna Finchen

Technical Editors
  Naheed Shaikh

  Vishal D'souza

Project Coordinator
  Michelle Quadros

Proofreader
  Elinor Perry-Smith

Indexer
  Hemangini Bari

Production Coordinator
  Prachali Bhiwandkar

Cover Work
  Prachali Bhiwandkar

About the Author

Juan Pablo Novillo Requena started building PHP websites professionally in London right after finishing his University studies in 2006. He spent some time using Symfony and Ruby on Rails and in 2010, back in Spain, he created his first website with Drupal. His commitment with the Drupal Community started a year later once he discovered how much fun and challenging it was to contribute. Currently, he maintains several modules such as Twitter and Oauth among others, he frequently submits and reviews patches for other projects (recently Drush), he participates in the Madrid and Spanish communities with talks and code sprints and overall he does his best to help Drupal evolve and get known to a wider audience.

Juan's Drupal profile can be found at `http://drupal.org/user/682736`.

I would like to thank Lorena for her everyday support in my career and life. My family for believing in me and for being so helpful. Also, thanks to my colleague Tushar Mahajan (`http://drupal.org/user/398572`), whose passion for Drupal and guidance was what got me into all this up to a level I could not even imagine.

About the Reviewer

Greg Anderson is one of the co-maintainers of Drush; he is the original author of site aliases and the sql-sync command. You can follow him at `http://twitter.com/greg_1_anderson`.

Jonathan Araña Cruz has been a sysadmin since early 2000 and has been involved with Drupal since 2006, when a site built by others fell in his hands. At present, he combines both sysadmin and Drupal development work. He has published some modules to aid migration from other CMS options to Drupal. He regularly contributes patches to modules he works with. At a point in time, he found Drush and saw a lot of possibilities in the management of Drupal from the command line. So, he started to contribute patches to improve Drush. Since 2010, he has been an official co-maintainer of the project.

Jonathan's Drupal profile can be found at `http://drupal.org/user/49817`.

www.PacktPub.com

Support files, eBooks, discount offers and more

You might want to visit www.PacktPub.com for support files and downloads related to your book.

Did you know that Packt offers eBook versions of every book published, with PDF and ePub files available? You can upgrade to the eBook version at www.PacktPub.com and as a print book customer, you are entitled to a discount on the eBook copy. Get in touch with us at service@packtpub.com for more details.

At www.PacktPub.com, you can also read a collection of free technical articles, sign up for a range of free newsletters and receive exclusive discounts and offers on Packt books and eBooks.

http://PacktLib.PacktPub.com

Do you need instant solutions to your IT questions? PacktLib is Packt's online digital book library. Here, you can access, read and search across Packt's entire library of books.

Why Subscribe?

- Fully searchable across every book published by Packt
- Copy and paste, print and bookmark content
- On demand and accessible via web browser

Free Access for Packt account holders

If you have an account with Packt at www.PacktPub.com, you can use this to access PacktLib today and view nine entirely free books. Simply use your login credentials for immediate access.

Table of Contents

Preface

Drush is a command line interface for Drupal. Most of the tasks for building and maintaining a website are repetitive and involve filling in forms on administration pages. The majority of these tasks can be achieved with a single Drush command, drastically shortening the development and maintenance time of a project.

What this book covers

Chapter 1, Installation and Basic Usage, starts with a couple of jaw-dropping examples, followed by an introduction to Drush, and then focuses on installation, usage, and some basic concepts.

Chapter 2, Executing Drush Commands, shows how common site-building and administration tasks in Drupal projects can be performed faster and easier using Drush commands, right after it has been installed. In order to demonstrate this, a sample Drupal project will be installed, configured, extended, monitored, and tested using Drush commands.

Chapter 3, Customizing Drush, dives into advanced topics such as writing and altering commands, executing scripts, working with site aliases and configuration files, and customizing our terminal.

Chapter 4, Extending Drush, expands the Drush toolkit by installing and testing contributed modules which implement new Drush commands.

What you need for this book

To run the examples in the book, the following software will be required:

- Operating system:

  Any Unix-based system such as:

  - Ubuntu (any version)
  - MAC OS X (any version)

  Alternatively, Windows XP or higher.

- Software:

  - PHP 5.2 or higher
  - MySQL 5.0 or higher
  - Apache 2.0 or higher
  - Drupal 7 (recommended)
  - Git

#	Software Name	URL
1	Ubuntu	http://www.ubuntu.com/
2	MAC OS X	http://www.apple.com/macosx
3	PHP	http://www.php.net/
4	MySQL	http://www.mysql.com/
4	Apache	http://www.apache.org/
5	Drupal 7	http://drupal.org

Who this book is for

Drupal developers or themers who have already built a few Drupal sites and understand its web-based administration.

If you have not ever touched a terminal, this book is progressively paced starting with the structure of a command, and finishing with how to simplify complex commands that interact with remote servers. However, you should learn the basic terminal commands in order to move around, copy and manage directories, connect and interact with a database, log in to remote systems, and have basic PHP programming skills.

Conventions

In this book, you will find a number of styles of text that distinguish between different kinds of information. Here are some examples of these styles, and an explanation of their meaning.

Code words in text are shown as follows: "Let's start with a very simple command such as `core-status`, which prints configuration information about Drush."

A block of code is set as follows:

```
/**
 * Implementation of hook_drush_help_alter()
 * Adds an option "enable" to pm-download command.
 */
function autoenable_drush_help_alter(&$command) {
  if ($command['command'] == 'pm-download') {
    $command['options']['enable'] = "Enable the module
automatically.";
  }
}
```

When we wish to draw your attention to a particular part of a code block, the relevant lines or items are set in bold:

```
/**
 * Implementation of hook_drush_help_alter()
 * Adds an option "enable" to pm-download command.
 */
function autoenable_drush_help_alter(&$command) {
  if ($command['command'] == 'pm-download') {
    $command['options']['enable'] = "Enable the module
automatically.";
  }
}
```

Any command-line input or output is written as follows:

```
$ drush user-blocker --since="1970" en

Blocked 0 users                              [success]
```

When we wish to draw your attention to a particular part of a command-line input or output, the relevant lines or items are set in italics:

```
$ drush user-blocker --since="1970" en
```

Long commands that expand on more than one line have a backslash (\) at the end of each line, so they can be copied and pasted on a terminal. Windows users should replace these backslashes by carets (^). Here is an example:

```
$ drush site-install \
  --db-url=mysql://username:password@localhost/festival \
  --site-name=Festival \
  standard
```

New terms and **important words** are shown in bold. Words that you see on the screen, in menus or dialog boxes for example, appear in the text like this: "Open the Command Line Interface at **Start | Programs | Accessories | Command Prompt**".

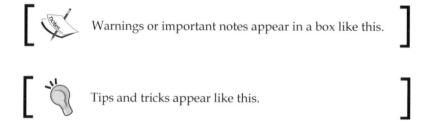

Warnings or important notes appear in a box like this.

Tips and tricks appear like this.

Reader feedback

Feedback from our readers is always welcome. Let us know what you think about this book—what you liked or may have disliked. Reader feedback is important for us to develop titles that you really get the most out of.

To send us general feedback, simply send an e-mail to feedback@packtpub.com, and mention the book title through the subject of your message.

If there is a topic that you have expertise in and you are interested in either writing or contributing to a book, see our author guide on www.packtpub.com/authors.

Customer support

Now that you are the proud owner of a Packt book, we have a number of things to help you to get the most from your purchase.

Downloading the example code

You can download the example code files for all Packt books you have purchased from your account at http://www.packtpub.com. If you purchased this book elsewhere, you can visit http://www.packtpub.com/support and register to have the files e-mailed directly to you.

Errata

Although we have taken every care to ensure the accuracy of our content, mistakes do happen. If you find a mistake in one of our books—maybe a mistake in the text or the code—we would be grateful if you would report this to us. By doing so, you can save other readers from frustration and help us improve subsequent versions of this book. If you find any errata, please report them by visiting http://www.packtpub.com/support, selecting your book, clicking on the **errata submission form** link, and entering the details of your errata. Once your errata are verified, your submission will be accepted and the errata will be uploaded to our website, or added to any list of existing errata, under the Errata section of that title.

Piracy

Piracy of copyright material on the Internet is an ongoing problem across all media. At Packt, we take the protection of our copyright and licenses very seriously. If you come across any illegal copies of our works, in any form, on the Internet, please provide us with the location address or website name immediately so that we can pursue a remedy.

Please contact us at copyright@packtpub.com with a link to the suspected pirated material.

We appreciate your help in protecting our authors, and our ability to bring you valuable content.

Questions

You can contact us at questions@packtpub.com if you are having a problem with any aspect of the book, and we will do our best to address it.

1
Installation and Basic Usage

Drush is a command-line shell and scripting interface for Drupal. It provides a set of commands which act as shortcuts to perform common tasks with Drupal sites. The purpose of this book is to explain Drush capabilities through practical examples. This chapter starts by showing some advanced examples and then focuses on installation, usage, and some basic concepts. The following chapters cover the command toolkit, customization, and extension.

These are the major things we will be covering in this chapter:

- How to install Drush in different operating systems
- The general syntax of a Drush command
- How to tell Drush which site we want it to work with

Introduction

Imagine the following scenario: you have been told to clear the cache of a website called http://somewebsite.com. Normally, this would involve the following steps:

1. Open the login form of that website in a web browser.
2. Enter the username and password of a user with administrative rights.
3. Navigate through **Administration** | **Configuration** | **Performance** and hit the button labeled as **Clear cache**.
4. Log out.

If you had Drush installed on your system, you would just need to open a terminal and execute the following command:

```
$ drush @somewebsite.com cache-clear all
```

That's it. You did not even have to provide user credentials. This little demonstration shows the potential that Drush has to simplify processes. Once you have configured Drush, you can do even cooler things such as downloading a database from a remote site to your local environment, excluding cache tables, and automatically resetting user e-mails and passwords with a command such as the following one:

```
$ drush sql-sync @somewebsite.com @somewebsite.local
```

Drush is a great tool to automate and speed up common tasks involving Drupal sites. If you have ever felt that you are doing the same thing many times, keep on reading to discover more effective ways to manage your Drupal sites!

Installation requirements

Drush can be installed manually or automatically, depending on your operating system and preferences. These are explained in this chapter through step by step instructions. You should evaluate them and, whichever you follow, make sure that you end up with Drush 4.5 or higher installed on your system.

Drush is designed for working on Unix-based systems such as Linux and Mac OS X. However, a lot of effort has been put into making some of its commands available in Windows systems.

 Windows users can install Ubuntu within VirtualBox to use Drush within a Unix-based environment. See http://www.ubuntu.com and https://www.virtualbox.org for more details.

Linux and Mac users need to verify that they can run PHP on the command line and its version is 5.2 or higher. If you are using Windows, you can jump to the next section as the Drush installer configures PHP automatically for your terminal. The easiest way to check whether you have PHP-CLI installed and configured, is by opening a terminal and executing the following command:

```
$ php -v
PHP 5.3.5-1ubuntu7.4 with Suhosin-Patch (cli)
  (built: Dec 13 2011 18:25:14)
Copyright (c) 1997-2009 The PHP Group
Zend Engine v2.3.0, Copyright (c) 1998-2010 Zend Technologies
```

If you got an output similar as the previous one, you can jump to the next section. If not, here are some tips to get PHP-CLI installed on your system.

Installing php-cli on Debian and Ubuntu

Debian and Ubuntu users can easily install `php-cli` with the following command:

```
$ sudo apt-get install php5-cli
```

Once the installation completes, verify the installed version with `php -v`.

Installing php-cli on Mac

Mac users have php-cli installed by default but need to make it available from anywhere in the terminal. The `whereis` command helps to find where a command is located. The following command shows how the `whereis` command is used to find where a command is located, if we have the PHP binary in our system:

```
$ whereis -b php
```

```
php: /usr/bin/php /usr/share/php /usr/share/man/man1/php.1.gz
```

If the command has found any results, as in the previous example, try executing them appending `-v` to see if the version is 5.2 or higher. If you have found it, create a symbolic link that points to any of the paths listed within your PATH environment variable. Now, in the future you can just type `php` instead of the full path where it's located. We will first print the available paths and then create a symbolic link to one of them:

```
$ echo $PATH
    /usr/local/sbin:/usr/local/bin:/usr/sbin:/usr/bin:/sbin:/bin:
/usr/games:/home/juampy/local/bin:/opt/android-sdk-linux_x86/tools
$ sudo ln -s /path/to/php/executable /usr/local/bin/php
```

After that, you should be able to run `php -v` without errors.

> You can find further information about requirements at the Drush README.txt (http://drupalcode.org/project/drush.git/ blob/HEAD:/README.txt).

Installation for Linux and Unix (including Mac)

Drush can be installed in Linux or Unix systems, manually or automatically, by a package management system such as PEAR, Aptitude, Port, Homebrew, and others (depending on your distribution). Although the automatic approach offers a quick and easy way to install Drush, there are some disadvantages:

- Some package management systems do not have Drush 4.5 available yet. For example, Ubuntu 11.04 installs Drush 4.4 through Aptitude.

- Drush may not be available at the official channels and you may need to add a *backports* channel in order to discover it. For example, the PEAR installation requires that you first install PEAR and then add the channel where Drush can be found and installed. Moreover, PEAR has to be installed previously and the installation process varies depending if you are using Linux or Mac.

- Some of them may not install everything in the right place. Aptitude installs Drush in Ubuntu without its documentation, so the `drush topic` command would not work.

After this reasoning, the most effective method is installing Drush manually, as it ensures that we are installing the correct release. Installing a previous version may result in some commands used in this book being made redundant, or unexpected results from other commands.

[For instructions on how to install Drush on shared hosting systems, read the contents of `http://drupal.org/node/1181480`.]

The installation process

1. In a web browser, open the Drush 4.5 release page at `http://drupal.org/node/1247086`.

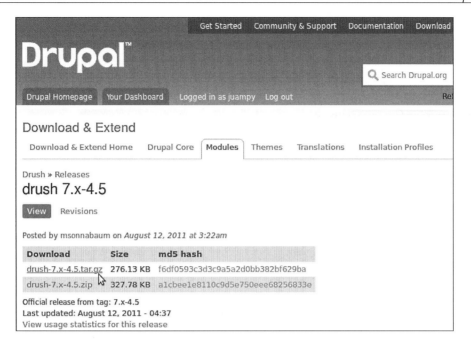

2. Download the **zip** or **tar.gz** to your home path. You can check where your home path is, with the following command:

   ```
   $ echo $HOME
   ```

   ```
   /home/juampy
   ```

3. Extract the contents of the compressed file. For `drush-7.x-4.5.tar.gz` use the following command:

   ```
   $ tar -zxvf drush-7.x-4.5.tar.gz
   ```

   ```
   drush/
   ```

   ```
   drush/examples/
   ```

   ```
   drush/examples/example.aliases.drushrc.php
   ```

   ```
   ...
   ```

> **Downloading the example code**
>
> You can download the example code files for all Packt books you have purchased from your account at http://www.packtpub.com. If you purchased this book elsewhere, you can visit http://www.packtpub.com/support and register to have the files e-mailed directly to you.

Alternatively, if you downloaded `drush-7.x-4.5.zip`, execute the following command to extract its contents:

```
$ unzip drush-7.x-4.5.zip
  Archive:  drush-7.x-4.5.zip
  creating: drush/
  creating: drush/examples/
```

...

4. Change directory to `drush`.

    ```
    $ cd /home/juampy/drush
    ```

5. Set permissions to the drush executable file in order to be able to run Drush with the following command:

    ```
    $ chmod u+x drush
    ```

6. Now try to execute it by typing its name:

    ```
    $ ./drush
    Execute a drush command. Run `drush help [command]` to
     view command-specific help.  Run `drush topic` to read even
     more documentation.
    ```

    You should see the Drush help as shown in the previous output.

7. Create a symbolic link of the Drush executable to any of the directories listed at your PATH environment variable; so you do not have to type `/home/juampy/drush/drush` every time you use it. Note that this command will ask you for your administrator password in order to proceed:

    ```
    $ echo $PATH
    /usr/local/sbin:/usr/local/bin:/usr/sbin:/usr/bin:/sbin:/bin:
    /usr/games:/home/juampy/local/bin:
    /opt/android-sdk-linux_x86/tools
    $ sudo ln -s /home/juampy/drush/drush /usr/local/bin/drush
    ```

8. Verify the installation by going to another directory and running `drush`:

    ```
    $ cd /home/juampy
    $ drush
    ```

    You should see an output similar to the one in step 6. Now you can start using Drush in your Drupal projects.

Installation on Windows

Drush 4 does not support Windows. However, there is an automatic installer for Drush 5. Although it does not have a stable release yet, it has all the capabilities of Drush 4.5. Hence, it is the preferred installation method in this case.

In case you experience problems using the installer, the manual installation process is explained as well in this section.

 Drush on Windows supports three shells: DOS, PowerShell, and msysgit (mingw). Cygwin is not formally supported, but is very similar to msysgit and should work.

Automatic installation

Drush has a Windows installer that sets up everything you need to start using Drush. The process is very similar to installing any other software in Windows.

Here are the steps to get it working:

1. Download the installer and the **Installation Guide** from `http://www.drush.org/drush_windows_installer`.

2. Open the **Installation Guide** and follow instructions to install Drush.

3. Once the installation completes, you can open a Drush terminal from the Windows Start menu. A shortcut on your desktop has been set up as well.

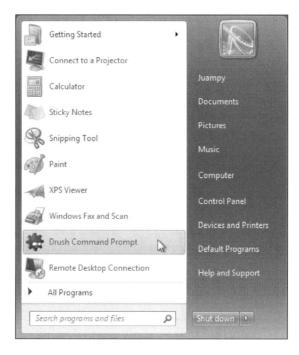

4. Both shortcuts open a Windows console configured to work with Drush. You can execute Drush commands there by typing `drush`.

5. If, when you enter `drush` and you get the error **php.exe could not be found**, run PHP manually and then try again, as in the following example:

```
C:\> php -v
C:\> drush
```

You should see now the list of commands and options for Drush.

Manual installation

The alternative installation method requires knowledge of the Windows system variables configuration and administrative permissions to replace a Windows library. The result has Drush 5 installed and works as the automatic installer does.

Installing required libraries

Drush needs a few libraries to be installed in order to work correctly. Take into account the following tips prior to installing them:

- Each installer can be found in their home pages at the first setup link of the **Download** section.

- When you open an installer, you may see up to three security warnings, as shown in the following screenshot, before the installation starts. Accept them, as these libraries should not involve any risk for your system.

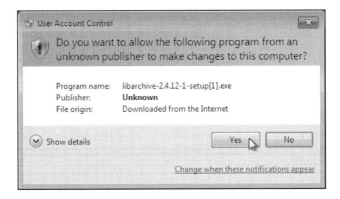

- During the installation process, leave all options with their default values and accept the terms of use.

Here are the home pages of each of the libraries:

- `http://gnuwin32.sourceforge.net/packages/libarchive.htm`
- `http://gnuwin32.sourceforge.net/packages/gzip.htm`

- `http://gnuwin32.sourceforge.net/packages/wget.htm`
- `http://gnuwin32.sourceforge.net/packages/gtar.htm`

Replacing the TAR Library

Now, we will replace the Windows Tar library (`tar`) with the one we just installed, by performing the following steps:

1. Open the file explorer and browse to the folder `C:\Program Files\ GnuWin32\bin\`.
2. Rename the file `tar` to `tar_default`. If Windows asks you to confirm this operation, accept it.
3. Make a copy of the file `bsdtar` (located in the same directory) and rename the copy to `tar`. If you can see the file extensions, keep them.
4. Your `bin` folder should look as shown in the following screenshot, after doing this.

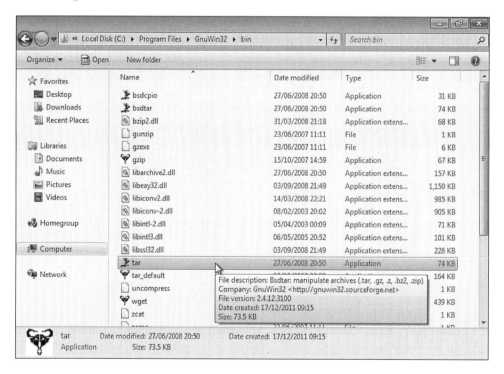

Installing Drush

In a web browser, open the Drush Project page and download the **zip** package of the **All-versions-5.x-dev** release: `http://drupal.org/project/drush`.

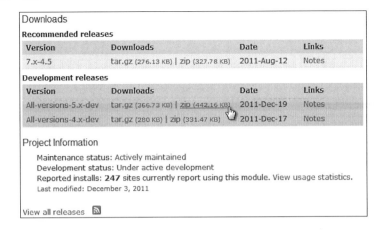

Extract the contents of the `zip` file to the root of your C drive, so `drush.bat` can be reached at `C:\drush\drush.bat`.

Configure environment variables

Configure your `Path` system variable by going to **My Computer** | **Properties** | **Advanced System Settings** | **Environment Variables**. At the **System Variables** list, double-click on **Path** and append this at the end of the **Variable value** field: **;C:\ php;C:\drush;C:\Program Files\GnuWin32\bin**.

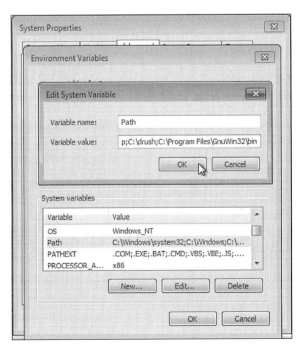

As you can see, we are providing the **Path** variable with the location of the PHP, Drush, and libraries directories. Make sure that these paths are correct as in some installations they may vary (for example, WAMP installs PHP at C:\wamp\bin\php and some Windows versions have **Program Files (x86)** instead of **Program Files**). Save the value and close all the windows you opened for doing this.

Verify the installation

Open the command-line interface at **Start | Programs | Accessories | Command Prompt**. If you had it already opened, then close and open again so it loads the new configuration. Once in, type the following:

```
C:\> drush core-status
```

```
PHP configuration      :  C:\php\php.ini
Drush version          :  5.0-dev
Drush configuration    :
Drush alias files      :
```

If you did not get the previously shown output, try to identify the error with the message reported or find more debugging information at http://drupal.org/node/594744.

Configuring php.ini

If you use the default php.ini configuration file, you may encounter unexpected errors using Drush such as timeouts, errors not being shown, or functions not being found. This is because the default configuration of PHP is too restrictive. Therefore, we will first identify where it is and if is not shared with the web server, configure it. If it is, an alternative method to override some of its settings will be explained.

You can easily find the php.ini file being used by Drush with the core-status command:

```
$ drush core-status PHP
 PHP configuration    :  /etc/php5/cli/php.ini
```

Now, in order to find out if the web server uses this file, create a file called info.php in a directory visible by your web server:

```
<?php
phpinfo():
```

Now open it in a web browser and look for the line **Loaded Configuration File**:

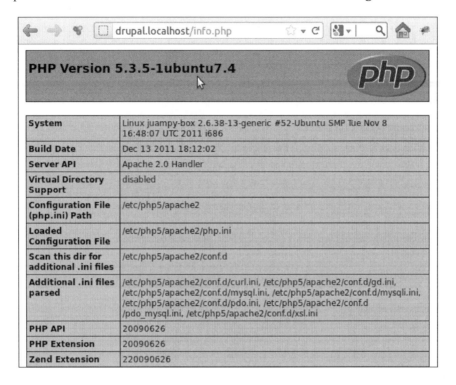

 If you created the info.php file in a public web server, do not forget to delete it.

If the file path is different from the one that drush core-status PHP reported, you are safe to go ahead configuring it. If not, create a php.ini file within the Drush installation directory (for example, at /home/juampy/drush/php.ini) with the following contents:

```
memory_limit = 128M
error_reporting = E_ALL | E_NOTICE | E_STRICT
display_errors = stderr
safe_mode =
open_basedir =
disable_functions =
disable_classes =
```

These settings make sure that Drush has enough memory to run; errors are printed onscreen and some PHP variables do not restrict it.

Drush command structure

Drush ships with a set of grouped commands to perform different tasks. If you are fluent at executing commands in the terminal, you can skip this section and start exploring the details of each Drush command in the next chapter. If not, you should understand what arguments and options are to a command and how they affect its behavior.

Executing a command

Let's start with a very simple command such as `core-status`, which prints configuration information about Drush and, if applicable, a Drupal site. If executed at the root of a Drupal directory with its database configured at `sites/default/settings.php`, the following command would return:

```
$drush core-status
Drupal version         :  7.4
Site URI               :  http://drupal7.localhost
Database driver        :  mysql
Database hostname      :  localhost
Database username      :  root
Database name          :  drupal7
Database               :  Connected
Drupal bootstrap       :  Successful
Drupal user            :  Anonymous
Default theme          :  bartik
Administration theme   :  seven
PHP configuration      :  /etc/php5/apache2/php.ini
Drush version          :  4.5
Drush configuration    :
Drush alias files      :
Drupal root            :  /home/juampy/myDrupalSite
Site path              :  sites/default
File directory path    :  sites/default/files
```

This output is informing us the main configuration of our site and Drush, which is its default behavior. Now, we can print its help information to find out that it can actually do more than that:

```
$ drush help core-status
Provides a birds-eye view of the current Drupal installation, if any.
Examples:
  drush status version              Show all status lines that
                                    contain version information.

  drush status --pipe               A list key=value items
                                    separatedby line breaks.
```

```
drush status drush-version--pipe          Emit just the drush version
                                          with no label.

Arguments:
  item                                    Optional.  The status item
                                          line(s) to display.

Options:
  --show-passwords                        Show database password.

Topics:
  docs-readme                             README.txt

Aliases: status, st
```

As we can see, the `core-status` command accepts arguments and options when being called. We will now see how to use them.

Providing arguments to a command

An **argument** is a piece of information that acts as input data for a command. They are typed next to the command name and separated by spaces.

The help information of the `core-status` command (type `drush help core-status` to see it again) says that we can specify the items which we want it to print. Therefore, if we need to print just the items containing `version` in the item name, we could do the following:

```
$ drush core-status version
Drupal version         :   7.10
Drush version          :   4.5
```

You can try and change `version` by something else or even add more parameters after it, so the command will print items containing them as well. If we wanted version and database information to be printed, the following command would do it:

```
$ drush core-status version database
Drupal version          :   7.10
Database driver         :   mysql
Database hostname       :   localhost
Database username       :   root
Database name           :   drupal7db
Database                :   Connected
Drush version           :   4.5
```

You can give any number of arguments to a command. Beware that some commands expect the arguments to be given in a certain order. For example, the command `variable-set` expects that the variable name to be set is the first argument and its new value is the second argument.

Hence, the following example sets the variable `site-name` with the value
`My Drupal site`:

```
$ drush variable-set site_name "My Drupal site"
```

Modifying a command's behavior through options

Drush commands accept options, which modify their default behavior. If, for
example, we wanted to list the database connection details of a Drupal site, we
would do the following:

```
$ cd /path/to/drupal/root/
$ drush core-status --show-passwords database
```

```
Database driver         :  mysql
Database hostname       :  localhost
Database username       :  root
Database name           :  drupal7site
Database password       :  drupal7sitePassword
Database                :  Connected
```

The option `--show-passwords` is telling Drush that we want to see the database
password of the site where we currently are. This option is needed because, by
default, the `status` command does not show database passwords.

Here is a full command that prints version and database information with database
passwords in a *key=value* format. Its full syntax is detailed as follows:

```
$ drush    core-status    --show-passwords --pipe    version database
           command        options                    arguments
```

As you can see, options are given after the command name and arguments are given
at the end. You can actually change the order and even mix them, but for clarity we
will follow the given structure.

In order to read the description and available arguments and options for a command,
use `drush help` and append to it the command name as an argument, such as:

```
$ drush help core-status
```

In the previous example, `core-status` is not a command but an argument for
the help command telling it that we want to see help information about the
`core-status` command.

Most of the Drush options have a short and long format and they may accept a value too. You can see if an option has a short format in the command help. As an example, if we wanted to tell a Drush command the URL of our site, we could do it in two ways. Here is the short one:

```
$ drush cache-clear -l drupal7.localhost all
```

And this is the long one:

```
$ drush cache-clear --uri=drupal7.localhost all
```

In this book, we will use the long format as it makes clearer the difference between option values from arguments.

There are some options which are applicable to most Drush commands. You can see a list of these using the following command:

```
$ drush topic core-global-options
```

Command aliases

Most of the Drush commands have a shorter alias to help us type less. You can see them between parenthesis next to each command name. Therefore, the following command $ drush status is a shortcut for $ drush core-status.

For clarity, we will not use command aliases in this book, but you should learn and use them. Here is an example showing a portion of the help information of the core-status command where its aliases are listed in parenthesis.

```
$ drush help core-status
...
core-status (status, st)   Provides a birds-eye view of the current Drupal
installation, if any
...
```

This means that the three following commands give the same result:

```
$ drush core-status
$ drush status
$ drush st
```

Telling Drush which site to work with

Some Drush commands are to be executed on a non-Drupal directory (for example, site-install), others behave differently when executed on a Drupal directory (such as pm-download), and the remaining ones must be called within or referencing a Drupal directory (sql-connect). Here, we will explain how to tell Drush explicitly or implicitly that we want it to work with a Drupal site in particular.

Drush gathers information from arguments, options, and configuration files, creating a **context**.

The recommended method for working with Drush, against a Drupal site, is to run all commands from the root path of the site (where the index.php file is). This means that if, for example, a Drupal site is installed at /var/www/drupal7/ and its settings file is located at /var/www/drupal7/sites/default/settings.php, you could clear the cache by doing the following:

```
$ cd /var/www/drupal7/
$ drush cache-clear
```

The previous command will work correctly because Drush realizes that we are at the root of a Drupal directory and will find a database configuration at sites/default/settings.php. However, if we were using the multi-site feature of Drupal, settings.php would not be at sites/default, but at something such as sites/drupal7.localhost. In this scenario, we can still run commands easily by placing ourselves at the same level of the settings.php. This means the following commands:

```
$ cd /var/www/drupal7/sites/drupal7.localhost
$ drush cache-clear
```

This command works because Drush finds a settings.php file right where we are. If we would have tried to clear the cache from the root path (/var/www/drupal7/) as in the previous example, Drush would have printed an error:

```
$ cd /var/www/drupal7
$ drush cache-clear
```

```
The drush command 'cache-clear' could not be executed.          [error]
Could not find a Drupal settings.php file at ./sites/default/settings.
php.                        [error]
```

This command fails because Drush looks for `/var/www/drupal7/sites/default/settings.php` with no success. It does not have a database to clear its cache, and hence fails. To overcome this, we can make use of explicit methods to help Drush find our site, as explained in the next section.

 If you do not know how the Drupal multi-site feature works, read about it at `http://drupal.org/documentation/install/multi-site`.

Explicit methods

By informing Drush where the root path is and the site name within sites subdirectory, we can execute commands from any directory. For example, if our Drupal root path is located at `/var/www/drupal7` and the `settings.php` is in a different directory than `sites/default` (which happens on multi-site installations), then we could invoke the command from the Drupal root path specifying the site name as an option:

```
$ cd /var/www/drupal7
$ drush cache-clear --uri=drupal7.localhost
```

We can even go one step further and clear the cache of our Drupal site without even being at the root path by running the following commands:

```
$ cd /home/juampy
$ drush cache-clear --root=/var/www/drupal7 --uri=drupal7.localhost
```

This command is saying "Hey Drush, I want you to clear the cache of a Drupal site which has its root path at `/var/www/drupal7` and its `settings.php` at `/var/www/drupal7/sites/drupal7.localhost`".

Whenever you want to check the current active context, you can make use of the `core-status` command. See the following example, where it is executed in a non-Drupal directory:

```
$ cd /home/juampy
$ drush core-status

PHP configuration        :  /etc/php5/apache2/php.ini
Drush version            :  4.5
Drush configuration      :
Drush alias files        :
```

You can see that Drush just prints its version info and the location of the loaded `php.ini` configuration file. Now, we are going to run `drush core-status` from the root of a Drupal directory with its `settings.php` file located at `sites/default`:

```
$ cd /home/juampy/myDrupalSite
$ drush core-status

Drupal version            :  7.4
Site URI                  :  http://drupal7.localhost
Database driver           :  mysql
Database hostname         :  localhost
Database username         :  root
Database name             :  drupal7
Database                  :  Connected
Drupal bootstrap          :  Successful
Drupal user               :  Anonymous
Default theme             :  bartik
Administration theme      :  seven
PHP configuration         :  /etc/php5/apache2/php.ini
Drush version             :  4.5
Drush configuration       :
Drush alias files         :
Drupal root               :  /home/juampy/myDrupalSite
Site path                 :  sites/default
File directory path       :  sites/default/files
```

As you can see in the previous example, Drush discovers the site and prints its configuration details.

Drush incorporates a killer feature to provide all the information needed to run a command against a Drupal site from any directory with just one parameter (for example, drush `@mysite core-status`). It is called **Drush site alias** and it is explained in *Chapter 3, Customizing Drush*. There is another way of doing this which is with **Drush configuration files**, which will be explained as well.

Summary

After reading this chapter, you are ready to blast off. You have installed Drush and its software requirements and know how to do it in other operating systems. You tested some commands and understood how to use options and arguments with them. Finally, you found out that you can move around directories and still execute commands towards a particular Drupal site.

In the next chapter, you will discover what each Drush command can do with a practical example.

2
Executing Drush Commands

This chapter shows how common site-building and administration tasks in Drupal projects can be performed faster and easier using Drush commands, right after it has been installed. In order to demonstrate this, a sample Drupal project will be installed, configured, extended, archived, restored, and monitored using Drush commands. Get ready to dive into the terminal and start typing rather than clicking!

Downloading and installing Drupal (site-install)

We are about to download the latest Drupal 7 version available, to be the foundation of our test project. Let's call it Festival: a site to promote our favorite music festival.

 Almost everything in the rest of the chapter is compatible with Drupal 6. Whenever there is a difference, it will be pointed out.

The first thing we need to do is to download Drupal core into a directory which will be our root path. Here is an example of how to achieve it:

```
$ cd /home/juampy/projects
$ drush pm-download --drupal-project-rename=festival drupal
Project drupal (7.10) downloaded to              [success]
  /home/juampy/projects/festival.

Project drupal contains:          [success]
  - 3 profiles: minimal, standard, testing
  - 4 themes: seven, stark, garland, bartik
```

```
  - 47 modules: simpletest, shortcut, text, list, number, field_
sql_storage, options, field, forum, node, help, contact, php, book,
aggregator, dashboard, toolbar, syslog, taxonomy, user, filter, rdf,
dblog, menu, path, translation, comment, field_ui, color, trigger,
locale, openid, statistics, search, contextual, blog, block, poll,
update, file, overlay, image, profile, system, tracker, drupal_system_
listing_incompatible_test, drupal_system_listing_compatible_test
```

The pm-download command outputs a description of what version it has downloaded and its contents. We have used the --drupal-project-rename option to rename the generated directory from drupal-7.10 to festival.

Now, we are going invoke the Drupal installation process. Without even opening the browser and just by typing one Drush command we will obtain:

- A database called festival with the basic data for our site defined by an installation profile called standard
- The sites/all/settings.php file configured and pointing to a database
- The sites/all/files directory ready to be used by the website

First we will execute it, and then we will go through its syntax and output in detail. Note that you have to replace the username and password strings in the command with an existing MySql's username and password (normally, this is the root user for local development environments):

```
$ drush site-install \
  --db-url=mysql://username:password@localhost/festival \
  --site-name=Festival \
  standard
You are about to DROP your festival database and then CREATE a new one.
Do you want to continue? (y/n):
```

Unless you already have a database with the name festival, you can safely accept the warning. This will start the installation process:

```
Starting Drupal installation. This takes a few seconds …          [ok]
```

This command installs a Drupal site in our system. We provided with it the following arguments and options:

- A MySQL database connection string that the command will forward to the installation process in order to create and configure the database.
- The site name (Festival). If not given, our site would be called "Drupal".

- An installation profile name. Drupal core comes with three installation profiles: **Minimal**, **Standard**, and **Testing**. We have chosen the **Standard** installation profile as it configures the most common features of a Drupal site. Custom or contributed installation profiles can be placed in the `profiles` directory to be used instead.

Once the process completes, we only need to configure our web server so a local URL (for example, `http://festival.localhost`) that resolves to the root directory of our project (which is `/home/juampy/projects/festival` for this example). It is outside of the scope of this book to instruct you how to do it, but, in case you need it, you can find a lot of useful information at `http://drupal.org/node/157602`. Once you have set it up, open your web browser, type `http://festival.localhost` in the URL address field and hit *Enter*. Here is an example of how our website looks like when opening it for the first time:

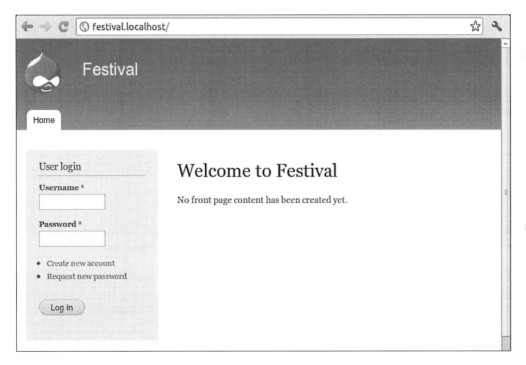

The site's homepage is presented. You can log in as the administrator by typing *admin* in both the **Username** and **Password** fields at the **User login** form.

`site-install` has plenty of options available. Here are some command examples and a description of what their output would be:

- Download the Spanish Drupal core translation, install Drupal with Spanish as the default language and Spain as the default country using `sites/drupal.localhost` instead of `sites/default` for the site configuration:

```
$ wget -O profiles/standard/translations/drupal-7.10.es.po \
 http://ftp.drupal.org/files/translations/7.x/drupal/drupal-7.10.
es.po
```

```
$ drush site-install \
  --db-url=mysql://username:password@localhost/drupal \
  --site-name="Spanish Festival" \
  --locale=es \
  --sites-subdir=drupal.localhost standard \
  install_configure_form.site_default_country=ES
```

- Provide specific details for the `admin` account:

```
$ drush site-install \
  --db-url=mysql://username:password@localhost/drupal \
  --account-name="Webmaster" --account-pass="W3bm4st3Drpl" \
  --account-mail="webmaster@drupal.localhost" standard
```

- Specify a MySQL account with higher privileges to create the database (for example, the MySQL root user account):

```
$ drush site-install \
  --db-url=mysql://username:pass@localhost/drupal \
  --db-su=root --db-su-pw=rootPassword standard
```

Configuring a site (variable-set and variable-get)

Once logged in as the administrator in our newly created site, it is time to configure its basic behavior. We could navigate through each of the configuration pages, choosing what best fits our purpose. However, there are some scenarios where you know which settings you want to set and do not want to go log in and go through each of the configuration pages, where they are located, to change them. For example, imagine that you have just downloaded a production database, and every time you do this you have to change a few settings to block unwanted reactions while working with the site (such as disabling SMTP e-mail submission). The commands `variable-set`, `variable-get`, and `variable-delete` allow you to configure, view, and delete Drupal configuration variables stored at the `variable` table.

Listing available variables

First of all, let's see what variables are already set in the variable table of our site's database:

```
$ cd /home/juampy/drupal
$ drush variable-get
admin_theme: "seven"
clean_url: TRUE
comment_page: 0
cron_key: "zRL-wZQLsgnh0JXkjs3tylQkmvFxRwF-tnH88nUWWs8"
cron_last: 1324731815
css_js_query_string: "lwpllz"
date_default_timezone: "Europe/London"
drupal_http_request_fails: FALSE
...
```

The list is not too long, but, that is because Drupal only sets the most important ones during installation. The rest will use their default values, which are provided when calling the function `variable_get()`. If you list the variables of a mature site, you will see many more.

You can filter which variables you want to see by giving part of the variable name as an argument to the command. For example, we could list all the user-related variables such as this:

```
$ drush variable-get user
user_admin_role: "3"
user_email_verification: "0"
user_pictures: "1"
user_picture_dimensions: "1024x1024"
user_picture_file_size: "800"
user_picture_style: "thumbnail"
user_register: "1"
```

Setting new values to variables

A very common use case with the `variable-set` command is to use it to turn on and off Drupal's **Maintenance mode**. This mode is set through a variable and it is very easy to manipulate its value without having to log in as the administrator and set it in the administration interface. Here is how we can turn on maintenance mode in a Drupal site with a command:

```
$ cd /home/juampy/projects/drupal
$ drush variable-set maintenance_mode 1
Enter a number to choose which variable to set.
  [0]  :  Cancel
  [1]  :  maintenance_mode (new variable)
1
maintenance_mode was set to 1.                [success]
```

The command printed two options: one for canceling the action and other for creating a new variable called `maintenance_mode` with a value of 1. The fact is that if a site has never been set to maintenance mode, the variable does not exist and that is why the new variable text appears. Try to open your Drupal site to verify that it shows a maintenance message. If you want to turn it off, set the value of the variable to `0`:

```
$ drush variable-set maintenance_mode 0
Enter a number to choose which variable to set.
  [0]  :  Cancel
  [1]  :  maintenance_mode
1
maintenance_mode was set to 0.                [success]
```

 Drupal 6 users should use the variable name `site_offline` instead of `maintenance_mode`, as the latter is for Drupal 7.

Now let's set up a few more variables with new values. We will set up the following:

- The default time zone to be Madrid
- The default country to be Spain
- The administrator's e-mail to be a different e-mail account

Here is an example that illustrates how to achieve these requirements:

```
$ drush variable-set --always-set date_default_timezone "Europe/Madrid"
date_default_timezone was set to Europe/Madrid.          [success]
$ drush variable-set --always-set date_default_country "ES"
date_default_country was set to ES.             [success]
$ drush variable-set --always-set site_mail "admin@drupal.localhost"
site_mail was set to admin@drupal.localhost.          [success]
```

As you can see, it's a matter of providing the variable name and the desired value to the command. In order to bypass confirmation messages to change the variables, we have added the `--always-set` option.

Now, we are going to set variables that have not been set up yet (hence, they currently do not exist in the variables table). We first need to identify each variable name and the correct value, that we want from the page where it can be set in the administration panel of our Drupal site. Instead of filling it there, we are going to grab its name and do it from the command line. This way will teach you how to set other variables in the future. For this example, we are going to let anyone register on our site, and will not require the Administrator's approval for registered accounts. First, of all we need to identify the name and desired value of these two settings. Here is how:

1. Log in to your site as the administrator and open the account configuration at **Configuration | Account Settings**.

2. With a development tool such as Firefox's Firebug (`https://addons.mozilla.org/en-US/firefox/addon/firebug/`) or the built-in Chrome Developer Tools, inspect the radio option of **Visitors**, which is under **REGISTRATION AND CANCELLATION | Who can register accounts?**

A frame with this piece of HTML will appear at the bottom as shown in the following screenshot:

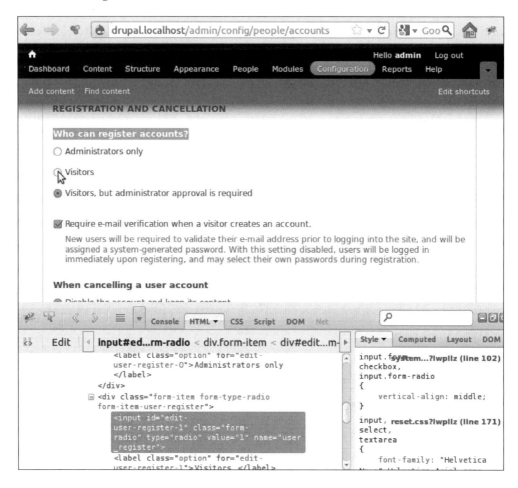

3. The following highlighted HTML code contains what we are looking for:

```
<input type="radio" class="form-radio" checked="checked" value="1"
name="user_register" id="edit-user-register-1">
```

4. You can see in the previous code that the attribute `name` has a value of `user_register` and the attribute `value` has a value of `1`. However, the checked radio is the third one (**Visitors, but administration approval is required**), which means that currently `user_register` has a value of `2`.

5. For the case of the **Require e-mail verification when a visitor creates an account.** checkbox, the following HTML code represents it:

```
<input type="checkbox" class="form-checkbox" value="1" name="user_
email_verification" id="edit-user-email-verification">
```

6. As we can see the attribute `name` has a value of `user_email_verification` and the attribute `value` has a value of `1`. This means that currently `user_email_verification` has a value of `1`.

7. We have identified the variables that we want to set. Now, we are going to change them: `user_register` will have a value of `1` in order to allow visitors to register in the site, and `user_email_verification` will have a value of `0` in order to disable e-mail verification on user registration. Let's see the values in the command line, update them, and then print their new values:

```
$ drush variable-get user_register
user_register: 2
$ drush variable-get user_email_verification
No matching variable found.                        [error]
$ drush variable-set --yes user_register 1
user_register was set to 1.                        [success]
$ drush variable-set --yes user_email_verification 0
user_email_verification was set to 0.              [success]
$ drush variable-get user_register
user_register: "1"
$ drush variable-get user_email_verification
user_email_verification: "0"
```

8. In the previous example, we have first checked the values of these variables. Note that `user_email_verification` did not even exist yet. This means that it was using the default value given by the source code and not from the database. Then, we set their values and printed them again to verify that they were changed. If you open the same page again in your browser, you will see that these settings have been updated accordingly in the configuration form. As you see, some knowledge of HTML forms is needed in order to find out the correct value of each variable.

 Features module and installation profiles are good strategies to configure Drupal sites, they are both covered in *Chapter 4, Extending Drush.*

Deleting variables

If we ever wanted to completely delete the value of a variable, we would use `variable-delete`. For example, if we need to delete the variable `user_email_verification` so it uses its default value again, then this would mean executing the following command:

```
$ drush variable-delete --yes user_email_verification
user_email_verification was deleted.          [success]
```

Finding variables by name

All `variable-x` commands will help you to find the desired variable if you just type part of its name. This means that you do not need to enter the exact variable name, as Drush will try to find all the variables that contain part of the argument given. For example, imagine that we want to change the `user_picture` dimensions to a smaller scale, but we are not sure which is the exact variable name:

```
$ drush variable-set user_picture "800x600"
Enter a number to choose which variable to set.
  [0]  :  Cancel
  [1]  :  user_picture (new variable)
  [2]  :  user_picture_dimensions
  [3]  :  user_picture_file_size
  [4]  :  user_picture_style
2
user_picture_dimensions was set to 800x600           [success]
```

This example demonstrates how Drush lists a set of options where you can either `Cancel` the operation (option 0), set the value to a new variable called `user_picture` (option 1), or set it to any of the others listed (options 2, 3, and 4). In this case, option 2 was the one we were looking for. Typing 2 and then pressing *Enter*, committed the `variable-set` command.

Working with projects (pm-X and user-X)

Drupal gets really interesting when plugging projects into it. A project can be a module, a theme, an installation profile, or a copy of Drupal core. The task of downloading, extracting, and enabling a project is one of the most common ones while building a site. Fortunately, Drush comes with a set of commands to help us work with modules effectively: the **Project Manager** commands. Let's start working with them through examples.

Viewing project information

`pm-releases` and `pm-releasenotes` are very useful tools for inspecting the details of a project prior to downloading it. In the following example, we will use `pm-releases` to list all available releases for the **Freelinking** module:

```
$ drush pm-releases --all freelinking
------- RELEASES FOR 'FREELINKING' PROJECT -------
 Release              Date            Status
 7.x-3.x-dev          2011-Sep-02     Development
 7.x-3.1              2011-Aug-19     Supported, Recommended
 7.x-3.0              2011-Aug-03
```

The previous command used the option `--all` to output all the releases and not just the most recent ones. For example, the last one in the list (`7.x-3.0`) does not have support and is older than `7.x-3.1`. The `--dev` option lists only development releases, as in the following example:

```
$ drush pm-releases --dev freelinking
------- RELEASES FOR 'FREELINKING' PROJECT -------
 Release              Date            Status
 7.x-3.x-dev          2011-Sep-02     Development
```

If we want to know what is in a project release, we can print its release notes by executing `pm-releasenotes`. Here is an example of how to print release notes about the latest release of the Freelinking module:

```
$ drush pm-releasenotes freelinking
------------------------------------------------
 > RELEASE NOTES FOR 'FREELINKING' PROJECT, VERSION 7.x-3.1:
 > Last updated: August 19, 2011 - 10:51 .
 > Supported, Recommended
------------------------------------------------
Official release from tag: 7.x-3.1
    *  #1247000: Getting freelinking to play nice with Media module
    *  #959832: Nodetitle rewrites link titles when the target node exists
    *  #1242090: Warning messages in Feelinking settings
```

When just the project name is given to `pm-releasenotes`, the command gathers information about the latest release. A specific version number can be given if needed, as in the following example:

```
$ drush pm-releasenotes freelinking-7.x-3.0

------------------------------------------------------------

 > RELEASE NOTES FOR 'FREELINKING' PROJECT, VERSION 7.x-3.0:

 > Last updated: August 3, 2011 - 08:01 .

------------------------------------------------------------

 Official release from tag: 7.x-3.0

 First stable version of freelinking 3 for Drupal 7.
```

Downloading and enabling modules

One of the must-have modules for almost every Drupal website is **Views**. We are going to download and enable it; but first we will create the directory to place contributed modules according to common good practice regarding module management described at `http://drupal.org/documentation/install/modules-themes/modules-7`:

```
$ cd /home/juampy/projects/drupal

$ mkdir sites/all/modules/contrib

$ drush pm-download views

Project views (7.x-3.0) downloaded to
/home/juampy/projects/drupal/sites/all/modules/contrib/views.
[success]

Project views contains 2 modules: views, views_ui.

$ drush pm-enable views views_ui

The following projects have unmet dependencies:

views requires ctools

views_ui requires ctools

Would you like to download them? (y/n):

y

Project ctools (7.x-1.0-rc1) downloaded to
/home/juampy/projects/drupal/sites/all/modules/contrib/ctools.
  [success]

Project ctools contains 9 modules: ctools_plugin_example, ctools_ajax_
sample, views_content, page_manager, bulk_export, ctools_custom_content,
stylizer, ctools_access_ruleset, ctools.
The following extensions will be enabled: views, views_ui, ctools
```

```
Do you really want to continue? (y/n):
y
ctools was enabled successfully.              [ok]
views_ui was enabled successfully.            [ok]
views was enabled successfully.               [ok]
```

Views module and its dependencies have been enabled. With just two commands, we did so much:

- Views module was downloaded to `sites/all/modules/contrib` through the command `drush pm-download views`. Drush detected that we had a `sites/all/modules/contrib` directory (the standard location for contributed modules) and placed the module contents there.

- When attempting to enable Views and the **Views User Interface** modules with `drush pm-enable views views_ui`, Drush realized that Views depends on **Ctools** and asked if we wanted to download it, to which we answered yes (y). Note that Drush can only figure this out when the module name matches with the project name.

- CTools was downloaded and before being enabled, Drush prompted asking us for confirmation (we could have appended `--yes` at the end of the command to bypass it). We replied yes (y), then hit *Enter*, and the three modules (`views`, `views_ui`, and `ctools`) were enabled in our site.

This task, without using Drush, would have meant to download the correct version of Views from its project page and extract it to `sites/all/modules/contrib`. Then, download and extract CTools and finally go to the **Modules** page at `admin/modules` in our site to enable these two.

Choosing a specific version of a project

Project releases at `http://drupal.org` follow a naming convention that is used to easily identify the type of support given and maturity, just by reading their name. The structure is [project name]-[Drupal core version]-[project version] (such as views-7.x-3.0). Here is an example that lists all available releases for Views module for Drupal 7. Note that if you are at the root of a Drupal site, you do not need to specify Drupal core version:

```
$ drush pm-download --select --all views

Choose one of the available releases:
  [0]  :  Cancel
  [1]  :  7.x-3.x-dev  -  2012-Jan-09  -  Development
```

```
[2]  :  7.x-3.0          -  2011-Dec-18  -  Supported,     Recommended
[3]  :  7.x-3.0-rc3      -  2011-Nov-16  -  Security
[4]  :  7.x-3.0-rc1      -  2011-Jun-17  -
[5]  :  7.x-3.0-beta3    -  2011-Mar-28  -
[6]  :  7.x-3.0-beta2    -  2011-Mar-26  -
[7]  :  7.x-3.0-beta1    -  2011-Mar-26  -
[8]  :  7.x-3.0-alpha1   -  2011-Jan-06  -
2
Project views (7.x-3.0) downloaded to /home/juampy/projects/drupal/sites/
all/modules/views.      [success]
```

We downloaded `views-7.x-3.0`. Here is an explanation of each part within the release name:

- Project name is the project unique identifier. This can be found at the URL of the project. In the previous example, the project name is `views`.

- Drupal core version is the Drupal version that this project supports. Unless a project supports just a specific version of Drupal, this normally is 6.x for Drupal 6 projects and 7.x for Drupal 7 projects.

- The project version is the actual version of the project. In the previous example, it is `3.0`.

Drush uses the project release name convention to search for the best release available or lists available releases based on your request. Let's see some examples:

- Download the latest development release of Drupal 8:

  ```
  $ drush pm-download drupal-8.x
  ```

  ```
  Project drupal (8.x-dev) downloaded to
     /home/juampy/projects/drupal-8.x-dev.      [success]
  ```

- Download Drupal 7.7:

  ```
  $ drush pm-download drupal-7.7
  ```

  ```
  Project drupal (7.7) downloaded to
  /home/juampy/projects/drupal-7.7.      [success]
  ```

- Download version 1.3 Organic Groups for my current Drupal site. Note that Drupal core version (for example, 7.x) has not been specified here, so it will be discovered by Drush by inspecting our current path:

  ```
  $ drush pm-download og-1.3
  ```

  ```
  Project og (7.x-1.3) downloaded to
     /home/juampy/projects/drupal/sites/all/modules/og.      [success]
  ```

- Download the latest version of Zen theme for Drupal 6:

```
$ drush pm-download zen-6.x

Project zen (6.x-2.1) downloaded to
   /home/juampy/projects/drupal/sites/all/themes/zen.    [success]
```

- List all available releases for Views module for Drupal 7 before downloading one. Note that if you are at the root of a Drupal site, you do not need to specify Drupal core version:

```
$ drush pm-download --select --all views

Choose one of the available releases:
   [0]   :   Cancel
   [1]   :   7.x-3.x-dev       -    2012-Jan-09   -   Development
   [2]   :   7.x-3.0           -    2011-Dec-18   -   Supported,
                                                      Recommended
   [3]   :   7.x-3.0-rc3       -    2011-Nov-16   -   Security
   [4]   :   7.x-3.0-rc1       -    2011-Jun-17   -
   [5]   :   7.x-3.0-beta3     -    2011-Mar-28   -
   [6]   :   7.x-3.0-beta2     -    2011-Mar-26   -
   [7]   :   7.x-3.0-beta1     -    2011-Mar-26   -
   [8]   :   7.x-3.0-alpha1    -    2011-Jan-06
2
Project views (7.x-3.0) downloaded to /home/juampy/projects/
drupal/sites/all/modules/views.    [success]
```

As you can see, there is plenty of flexibility to choose the version you want. However, you normally should not have to worry about it and just provide the project name to `pm-download` and Drush will do the rest for you.

Disabling and uninstalling modules

The Project Manager commands help us to disable and uninstall modules as well. Let's take the chance to review the list of installed modules and do some clean up in order to gain performance in our site:

```
$ drush pm-list --status=enabled
```

Package	Name	Type	Version
Chaos tool suite	Chaos tools (ctools)	Module	7.x-1.0-rc1
Core	Block (block)	Module	7.10
Core	Color (color)	Module	7.10

Core	Comment (comment)	Module	7.10
Core	Contextual links (contextual)	Module	7.10
...			
Core	*RDF (rdf)*	*Module*	*7.10*
Core	User (user)	Module	7.10
Views	Views (views)	Module	7.x-3.0
Core	Bartik (bartik)	Theme	7.10
Core	Seven (seven)	Theme	7.10

The **RDF** module is not needed in this project, so we are going to disable and uninstall it:

```
$ drush pm-disable --yes rdf
The following extensions will be disabled: rdf
Do you really want to continue? (y/n): y
rdf was disabled successfully.        [ok]
$ drush pm-uninstall --yes rdf
The following modules will be uninstalled: rdf
Do you really want to continue? (y/n): y
rdf was successfully uninstalled.        [ok]
```

The previous commands (pm-disable and pm-uninstall) removed the logic (disable) and the data (uninstall) from our site. This saved us from going to the modules list, checking the RDF module, hitting the **Save** button, and then going to the **Uninstall** tab and repeating the same task.

Viewing information about downloaded projects

At some point you may need to view which version of a module you have installed in a site, where it is located, or view its list of dependencies. The pm-info command extracts extended information about a project within a Drupal site and prints it onscreen. Here is an example where we print detailed information about the Views module:

```
$ drush pm-info views
  Project          :  views
  Type             :  module
  Title            :  Views
  Description      :  Create customized lists and queries from
                      your database.
  Version          :  7.x-3.1
  Package          :  Views
  Core             :  7.x
  Status           :  enabled
  Path             :  sites/all/modules/views
  Schema version   :  7301
  Files            :  handlers/views_handler_area.inc,
                      handlers/views_handler_area_result.inc, handlers/
views_handler_area_text.inc, handlers/views_handler_area_view.inc, ...
  Requires         :  ctools
```

Upgrading modules

Contributed modules are evolving all the time. It won't be long until you see the "There are available updates" alert while navigating through your Drupal site as an administrator. Upgrading a module manually, means the following steps:

1. Remove the old version of the module from the source code.

2. Download and extract the latest version from the project page and place it where the old version was.

3. Open `update.php` in a web browser as the administrator and run database updates, if the new version of the module has any.

4. Clear the cache.

These steps can be performed with Drush as well. In order to illustrate this, we are going to download and install an early version of the Devel module and then upgrade it to the latest version.

1. Download an old version of Devel module. We will ask Drush to list all the available versions for our site and pick one.

   ```
   $ drush pm-download --select --all devel
   Choose one of the available releases:
    [0]  :  Cancel
   ```

```
[1]  :  7.x-1.x-dev        -  2012-Jan-08    - Development
[2]  :  7.x-1.2            -  2011-Jul-22    - Supported,
                                               Recommended
[3]  :  7.x-1.1            -  2011-Jul-20    -  Security
[4]  :  7.x-1.0            -  2011-Jan-04    -
[5]  :  7.x-1.0-rc1        -  2010-Dec-06    -
[6]  :  7.x-1.0-beta2      -  2010-Apr-21    -
[7]  :  7.x-1.0-beta1      -  2010-Mar-19    -
[8]  :  7.x-1.0-alpha1     -  2010-Feb-02    -
8

Project devel (7.x-1.0-alpha1) downloaded to /home/juampy/
projects/drupal/sites/all/modules/contrib/devel        [success]
```

2. Now, we can enable it:

```
$ drush pm-enable --yes devel
The following extensions will be enabled: devel
Do you really want to continue? (y/n): y
devel was enabled successfully.        [ok]
```

3. Once enabled, we are going to upgrade it with the pm-update command. As we do not want Drupal core to be upgraded too, we will add the option --no-core to it. This command generates a backup for us automatically, in case something goes wrong:

```
drush pm-update --no-core devel
Checked available update data for 2 projects.        [status]


Update information last refreshed: Thu, 01/12/2012 - 02:17
Update status information on all installed and enabled Drupal
projects:
```

Name	Installed version	Proposed version	Status
Drupal core	7.10	7.10	Up to date
Devel	7.x-1.0-alpha1	7.x-1.2	SECURITY UPDATE available

```
Security updates will be made to the following projects:
Devel [devel-7.x-1.2]


Note: A backup of your project will be stored to backups directory
if it is not managed by a supported version control system.


Note: If you have made any modifications to any file that
```

```
belongs to one of these projects, you will have to migrate those
modifications after updating.


Do you really want to continue with the update process? (y/n): y


Project devel was updated successfully.
Installed version is now 7.x-1.2.


Backups were saved into the directory /home/juampy/drush-backups/
drupal/20120112012028/modules/devel.          [ok]


Finished performing updates.          [ok]


The following updates are pending:

devel module :


7003 - issue #813132: change schablon.com to white for krumo.


Do you wish to run all pending updates? (y/n): y
```

4. Done! We have upgraded Devel from version 7.x-1.0-alpha1 to 7.x-1.2. During the process, there was a prompt asking us to confirm the upgrade process and then a backup was made, Devel module got replaced by the latest version and one database update was performed. Now, it would be time to check that our system is working correctly and, if not, we could restore it to its previous status by using the generated backup.

Creating users and user roles

Creating users and assigning roles to them through Drush is really helpful when we do not want to fill all the required fields of the **Add User** form (especially those that make sense only for registration purposes). We only need to provide a username, an e-mail, and a password. Let's see how we can manage users with a practical example.

Start by creating, through the web interface, a simple content type called **Band**, which will represent the list of bands attending our music festival. We will then create roles and users to manage this content type through Drush. Here is an example of how the content type fields would look. We have even added an **Image** field for each band's image.

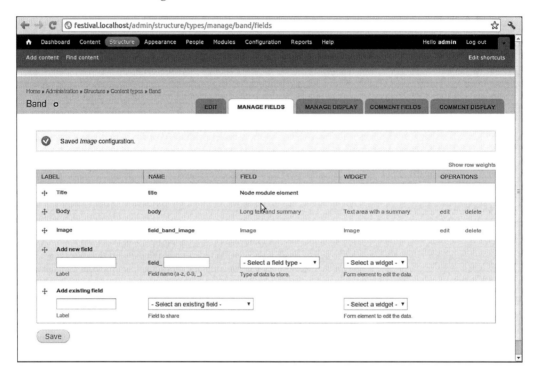

Then, as we know that there will be collaborators who will register bands in our site, we are going to create a role for them and then create a couple of users. First, we create a role **LINE-UP EDITOR** with all permissions for the **Band** content type, as in the following screenshot:

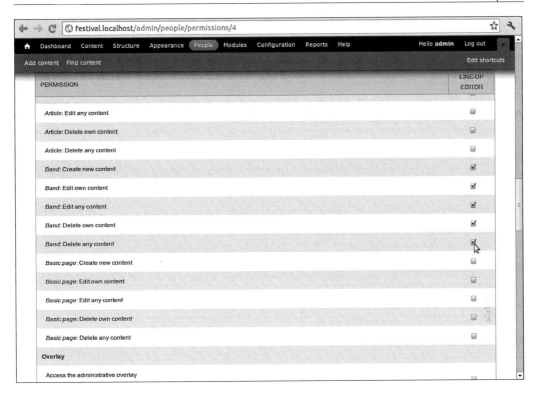

Having done that, we can create a user and assign it the `line-up editor` role:

```
$ drush user-create --mail="an_editor@festival.localhost"
  --password="editor" an_editor
  User ID      :  2
  User name    :  an_editor
  User mail    :  test@festival.localhost
  User roles   :  authenticated user
  User status  :  active
$ drush user-add-role "line-up editor" an_editor
Added the line-up editor role to uid 2          [success]
```

The first command (user-create) created the user. The second one (user-add-role) assigned the role line-up editor to it. Now, log in with the mentioned credentials and you will see that you can manage all content related to Bands.

The user commands offer us some really neat shortcuts to deal with the users of a Drupal site. Have a look at the following scenarios and possible solutions:

- Block a specific user:

  ```
  $ drush user-block anoying@user.com
  ```

- Unblock it:

  ```
  $ drush user-unblock anoying@user.com
  ```

- Change the password of the user with username houdini:

  ```
  $ drush user-password  --password=h4rderPaSSword houdini
  ```

- Reset the admin user password and open a one-time login screen in the web browser (note that the Drush command is surrounded by left back ticks):

  ```
  $ firefox `drush user-login --uri=drupal.localhost admin`
  ```

Clearing out cached data and image styles (cache-clear and image-flush)

Drupal's cache and image styles are very frequently recreated in the early stages of a project. On one hand, new menu entries are added, blocks are removed, and features are reverted among others. On the other, image styles are created and then modified several times so the images that use them suit new design requirements. These two can be cleared out with simple and very similar commands.

Flushing the cache

Clearing out the cache is one of the most common tasks in a Drupal site. Drupal has a few cache tables which share the same structure and are used to store data of a particular nature. Drush comes with a handy command for clearing out these tables: cache-clear. Without arguments, it prompts with the list of available cache types that can be cleared out:

```
$ cd /home/juampy/projects/drupal
$ drush cache-clear
Enter a number to choose which cache to clear.
  [0]  :  Cancel
```

```
[1]   :   all
[2]   :   theme registry
[3]   :   menu
[4]   :   css+js
[5]   :   block
[6]   :   module list
[7]   :   theme list
[8]   :   registry
[9]   :   views
9
'views' cache was cleared          [success]
```

In the previous example, we cleared the Views cache. As a shortcut, we can pass the cache type to the command itself:

```
$ drush cache-clear menu
'menu' cache was cleared                 [success]
$ drush cache-clear "theme registry"
'theme registry' cache was cleared          [success]
$ drush cache-clear all
'all' cache was cleared                     [success]
```

In production sites with a high demand of traffic, flushing all cache types could be catastrophic for the site's performance. Therefore, picking the right cache to clear in these scenarios is a wise practice.

Deleting generated images from an image style

An **image style** is used to generate different displays out of an image (for example, a thumbnail or an unsaturated version). It is very common to start a Drupal project and use the default image styles (thumbnail, medium, and small). However, once the theming process starts, these are normally modified to suit better needs. But what about all the images that were already uploaded to the site and thus generated through the existing image styles? Here is a practical scenario:

1. A view is created listing node images using the image style `thumbnail`.

2. A few nodes are created populating our list. It is looking good so far. All the thumbnails of our nodes are being generated at `sites/default/files/images/thumbnail`.

3. The designer kicks in, reviews the website, and yells, horrified! He/she starts theming the site and updates the `thumbnail` image style with a smaller scale.

4. Some of the pages which have images using the `thumbnail` image style are not reflecting this change. Here is how you could flush all these images:

```
$ drush image-flush thumbnail
Image style thumbnail flushed          [success]
```

If you want to clean all image styles in the system, pass the argument `all` to the command. You can also make it print a list of available options to choose from:

```
drush image-flush

Choose a style to flush.
 [0]   :  Cancel
 [1]   :  all
 [2]   :  thumbnail
 [3]   :  medium
 [4]   :  large
1
All image styles flushed          [success]
```

 Drupal 6 uses the contributed module **Imagecache**, which defines a couple of Drush commands that perform the same task as explained previously.

Running cron (core-cron)

Every Drupal site needs its cron task to be executed periodically. Depending on the activity of your site, you may want it to run once a day, every few hours, or every hour. Instead of relying on a web server to run cron (for example, using the command `wget http://drupal.localhost/cron.php`), Drush can execute it through the command line with the extra advantage of being able to use a PHP configuration file (`php.ini`) with a more suitable configuration.

 If you need further information about what cron does and different ways to set it up, there is plenty of documentation available at `http://drupal.org/documentation/modules/system` and `http://www.drush.org/docs/cron.html`

Here is an example of how to run cron with Drush:

```
$ cd /home/juampy/projects/drupal
$ drushcron
Cron run successfully.                              [success]
```

Working with a site's database (sql-X commands)

The SQL commands provide useful tools to perform common database tasks without the need of the database username and password, as Drush finds them for us. Any Drupal site's database can easily be inspected through a MySQL console with the `sql-connect` command. See the following example, where we connect to our database without the need of looking for and typing MySQL connection options in the command. Note that since the database configuration is located at `sites/all/settings.php`, Drush discovers it automatically. If this is not the case in your scenario, you should add the option `--uri=your_site_name` in order to tell Drush where the `settings.php` file is.

```
$ drush sql-cli
Reading table information for completion of table and column names
You can turn off this feature to get a quicker startup with -A

Welcome to the MySQL monitor.  Commands end with ; or \g.
Your MySQL connection id is 4304
Server version: 5.1.54-1ubuntu4 (Ubuntu)
Copyright (c) 2000, 2010, Oracle and/or its affiliates. All rights
reserved.
This software comes with ABSOLUTELY NO WARRANTY. This is free software,
and you are welcome to modify and redistribute it under the GPL v2
license

Type 'help;' or '\h' for help.Type '\c' to clear the current input
statement.
mysql> select uid, name from users;
+-----+------------+
| uid | name       |
+-----+------------+
| 0   |            |
```

```
|   1   |   admin      |
|   2   |   an_editor  |
+-------------------+

3 rows in set (0.00 sec)

mysql> exit

Bye
```

The Drush command `sql-connect` returns a MySQL connection string that can be used to pipe it to other commands. Here is an example of its basic execution:

```
$ drush sql-connect
mysql --database=drupal --host=localhost --user=root
  --password=somePass
```

`sql-connect` in conjunction with `sql-dump` can be used to load a database dump very easily. Imagine, that we want to extract a database dump from one site and load it into another. This could be done through the following steps:

1. Go to the root path of the site from which we want to extract a database dump:

   ```
   $ cd /home/juampy/projects/anotherDrupalSite
   ```

2. Generate a database dump and save it to `dump.sql`. This is the same as using the `mysqldump` command with the database name and user credentials.

   ```
   $ drush sql-dump > ../dump.sql
   ```

3. Change directory to the root path of the site where we want to load the database dump.

   ```
   $ cd /home/juampy/projects/drupal
   ```

4. Drop all existing tables in this database. You could bypass the confirmation message by appending the option `--yes` after the command name.

   ```
   $ drush sql-drop
   Do you really want to drop all tables? (y/n): y
   ```

5. Execute the output of `sql-connect` and use it to load the database dump. See that there are back ticks surrounding the Drush command. These back ticks mean that we want to execute the output of this command. In the previous example, you could see that `drush sql-connect` returns a MySql connection string. This is now used to connect to the database and load the database dump.

   ```
   $ `drush sql-connect` < ../dump.sql
   ```

6. The previous command is exactly the same as executing the following with `mysql`:

```
$ mysql --database=drupal --host=localhost --user=root \
    --password=drupalPassword < ../newDrupalSite/dump.sql
```

7. In order to clear out cached data from the other site, we clear out all caches.

```
$ drush cc all
'all' cache was cleared          [success]
```

Finally, the `sql-query` command allows single or batch queries from a file being executed against the site's database. This comes in handy to perform quick operations. Imagine that your manager asks you to block access to all users, except the administrator in a site. You could execute the following command to do it:

```
$ drush sql-query "update {users} set status=0 where uid <> 1"
```

You can also execute a batch of MySQL queries by providing a file to the command:

```
$ drush sql-query --input-file=example.sql
```

Backing up and restoring entire websites (archive-dump and archive-restore)

We have done some work on our site and it gets to the point where we start worrying about what would happen if something goes wrong and we lose everything, or if a change in the site will need a rollback that may be tedious. Drush provides a couple of commands to deal with this:

- `archive-dump`: This command packs a whole Drupal site including code, files, and database into a single file
- `archive-restore`: This command restores code, files, and database into a directory from a previous backup made with `archive-dump`

For example, let's create a directory out of our Drupal project where we will store our backups and then create one and place it there. Whenever you start to use this command on production environments, it is highly recommended that you copy these backups periodically to a safer machine, out of the server where the site runs.

```
$ cd /home/juampy
$ mdkir backups
```

```
$ cd projects/drupal
$ drush archive-dump
Archive saved to                                                    [ok]
/home/juampy/drush-backups/archive-dump/20120321213658/
drupal.20120321_093700.tar.gz
```

That's it. Note that if you want to backup a named site, you would have to specify it by appending it as an argument as shown in the following example:

```
$ drush archive-dump --destination=/home/juampy/backups/drupal.tar
  mysite.com
```

If we go to the backups directory, we will find the file drupal.tar. Go ahead and open it with a file compression software. This file contains the following:

- A directory with our project name that contains all the code, files, and configuration at the sites directory. If we had several sites configured and we specified them when we called archive-dump, these will be included in the backup. By default, if no arguments are defined, all sites are included.

- A database dump file with the name of our project plus the extension .sql containing the database dump of our site.

- A MANIFEST.ini that holds a structured description of the contents and properties of the backup. Here is an example of the one created by the previous command:

```
[Global]
datestamp = "1325108195"
formatversion = "1.0"
generator = "Drush archive-dump"
generatorversion = "4.5"
[default]
docroot = "/home/juampy/projects/drupal"
sitedir = "sites/default"
files-public = "sites/default/files"
database-default-file = "./drupal.sql"
database-default-driver = "mysql"
```

Now, we are going to restore our backup to another machine. Copy the drupal.tar file to another system, open a terminal, and execute the following command:

```
$ drush archive-restore drupal.tar
```

The command archive-restore will open the packaged file, read the MANIFEST.ini file, and perform the extraction and assembly of the contents into a new folder called drupal.

Monitoring watchdog messages (watchdog-X)

The `watchdog-x` commands allow us to list, view, and delete messages from the database log (visible at **Admin | Reports | Recent Log Messages**). Here is a description of each command:

- `watchdog-list` presents an interactive screen to list messages of a particular type or severity level
- `watchdog-show` prints all details of a particular message ID or lists latest messages based on several filtering options
- `watchdog-delete` is used to delete messages from the `watchdog` table. It also has filtering capabilities

Let's go through an example to explain these three commands. Imagine that we are facing an unexpected behavior with our implementation of `hook_user_insert` during user registration. At some point of the flow in our custom module, we have added the following `watchdog` call in order to verify something:

```
watchdog('custom_module', 'gotcha!');
```

After registering as a new user in our website, we can print the latest messages to see our output:

```
$ cd /home/juampy/projects/drupal
$ drush watchdog-show
```

Id	Date	Severity	Type	Message
56	29/Dec 14:52	notice	custom_module	gotcha!
55	29/Dec 14:52	notice	user	new user: testuser (test@test.com).
54	29/Dec 14:42	notice	user	Session opened for admin.
53	29/Dec 14:40	notice	user	Session opened for admin.
52	29/Dec 14:22	notice	user	Session closed for admin.
51	29/Dec 14:17	notice	user	Session opened for admin.
50	29/Dec 14:15	notice	cron	Cron run completed.
49	29/Dec 14:15	notice	user	Session opened for admin.

48	29/Dec 14:15	info	system	update module enabled.
47	29/Dec 14:15	info	system	update module installed.
46	29/Dec 14:15	notice	actions	Action 'Block current user' added.

The previous output lists the last 10 messages in descending order. It is fast and easy for quick verifications. However, there are times when we want to monitor this log over a period of time to see which new messages are arriving while we debug it. We can accomplish this by appending the `--tail` property to the `watchdog-show` command. This will query the `watchdog` table every second looking for new messages and printing them at the bottom:

```
$ drush watchdog-show --tail
```

46	29/Dec 14:15	notice	actions	Action 'Block current user' added.
47	29/Dec 14:15	info	system	update module installed.
48	29/Dec 14:15	info	system	update module enabled.
49	29/Dec 14:15	notice	user	Session opened for admin.
50	29/Dec 14:15	notice	cronCron run	completed.
51	29/Dec 14:17	notice	user	Session opened for admin.
52	29/Dec 14:22	notice	user	Session closed for admin.
53	29/Dec 14:40	notice	user	Session opened for admin.
54	29/Dec 14:52	notice	user	Session closed for admin.
55	29/Dec 14:52	notice	user	New user: testuser (test@test.com).
56	*29/Dec 14:52*	*notice*	*custom_module*	*gotcha!*

The latest 10 entries are listed now in ascending order and the cursor stays waiting for new messages. Now, if we create another user, two more entries will appear at the bottom:

57	29/Dec 14:55	notice	user	New user: anotheruser (test@drupal.local).
58	29/Dec 14:55	notice	custom_module	gotcha!

We can stop the command execution from querying for new messages by pressing together *Ctrl* and *C* keys.

Once we are done debugging, it is time to clear out the debug messages that we created by using the `watchdog-delete` command:

```
$ drush watchdog-delete --type=custom_module
All messages with type = custom_module will be deleted.
Do you really want to continue? (y/n): y
10 watchdog messages have been deleted.          [ok]
```

Before deleting, Drush informed us that it found 10 messages of this type and required our confirmation in order to proceed, to which we answered yes (y). You can make use of the `--type` and `--filter` options to select which messages you want to delete. The command also accepts the following arguments:

- A string contained in the message contents:

  ```
  $ drush watchdog-delete "gotcha!"
  ```

  Deletes all messages that contain the word "gotcha!".

- A message ID:

  ```
  $ drush watchdog-delete 56
  ```

  Deletes the message with ID 56.

- The token `all` to clear out the whole log:

  ```
  $ drush watchdog-delete all
  ```

  Deletes all messages.

Summary

We have gone through the majority of Drush commands. As you may have realized, they have many things in common. This will help you understand and make the most of new commands faster in the future. With the knowledge gained in this chapter, you are now able to deal with Drupal installations, module management, upgrades, cache and image clearing, user management, database handling, backups, tests, and monitoring much more effectively than through the Administration interface. Hopefully, you have also started to feel that the terminal is your friend and a tool to master, in order to progress even further.

In the next chapter, we will learn how to write our own Drush commands, configure Drush to load attributes and arguments automatically, execute commands in remote machines, and altering existing commands to fit our needs.

3
Customizing Drush

Drush is highly configurable. With the contents of this chapter and some practice you will feel that you are doing magic with your console. Imagine that you can download a whole production database ignoring cache tables, resetting user emails and passwords to your local database with just one short command such as `drush sql-sync @prod @local`. Yes, it is possible.

In this chapter, you will learn about the following topics:

- Write, test, and validate our first Drush command
- Altering and taking action when a command is executed
- Running PHP code directly on the command line or in PHP scripts after bootstrapping a Drupal site
- Create an alias for our testing Drupal site and issue commands to it
- Executing commands against remote systems and synchronizing files, code and databases
- Defining Drush configuration files for a user, a Drupal installation or a single site
- Optimizing our terminal in order to run even shorter commands

These are advanced topics which will need some systems administration skills such as knowing where your home path is, how to set up, and use **SSH** and how to authenticate against a remote host with a **Public Key**. Some Drush commands dealing with remote systems have limitations when being executed from Windows but workarounds will be explained in these cases.

Writing a custom command

So far you have seen most of the Drush command toolkit. Now it is time for us to think about how Drush can help us accomplish tasks that cannot be done with a few commands. Hence, it is time to write our own Drush command.

Here are some examples where you should choose to write a Drush command:

- To run a periodic task that needs to be completely isolated because it can take a long time to complete and therefore cannot be executed through Cron
- To extend the capabilities of an existing command in order to perform extra tasks needed in the production environments of your websites
- To perform a task without a graphic interface, such as the content generator command of the Devel module

Drush commands follow a syntax very similar to Drupal. They are defined within a hook as an array of properties and a callback function does the processing. They also have hooks before, during, and after their execution. These will be explained in the next section.

Commands in Drush have the following structure (based on `http://www.drush.org/docs/commands.html`):

- A file named `COMMANDFILE.drush.inc` where `COMMANDFILE` is the **namespace** of the group of commands that will be implemented
- An implementation of the hook `COMMANDFILE_drush_help()` which optionally describes each command and how they are categorized in the output of the `drush help` command
- An implementation of the hook `COMMANDFILE_drush_command()` where the basic properties of each command are defined
- A callback function for each defined command at `COMMANDFILE_drush_command()` that will do the actual processing following the function name `drush_COMMANDFILE_COMMANDNAME()`

Let's write a very simple but illustrative command. Imagine that we have a website where we need to block user accounts based on the following requirements:

1. By default, accounts which have not logged in during the last two years should be blocked (except the administrator account)
2. If languages are provided, then filter user accounts by these languages
3. If a period of time is given, then filter user accounts which logged in for the last time earlier than the one provided

Based on the previous requirements, we will create a custom command to perform these operations as the existing `user-block` command works only on specific users and cannot be extended to suit the previous requirements.

Writing our command

We are about to create the file where our command will reside. It is important that we carefully follow the structure COMMANDFILE.drush.inc so that Drush can discover it, and also that think about a good name for COMMANDFILE as Drush will use this part of the filename to invoke the callback function that will actually do the processing.

Custom Drush command files can be placed in several locations in our system:

- In a custom directory defined by the --include option or by a drushrc.php configuration file. More on **Using Configuration Files** later in this chapter.

- At the shared system commands, residing in $SHARE_PREFIX/share/drush/commands. For example, at /usr/share/drush/commands.

- In the $HOME/.drush folder, where $HOME is an environment variable that defines your home path. For example, /home/juampy/.drush/COMMANDFILE.drush.inc. This is the recommended location for general purpose commands, which we do not need to share with other users in the system.

For this scenario, we will go with the last option. We will create a file with the filename user_blocker.drush.inc inside the .drush folder within our home path (for example, at /home/juampy/.drush/user_blocker.drush.inc). This file has a hook for defining the command properties and a callback function that actually does the processing. The first part defines the command properties, such as the command description, examples, arguments, and options:

```php
<?php
/**
 * @file
 * Blocks users with no activity in a period of time
 */
/**
 * Implementation of hook_drush_command().
 */
function user_blocker_drush_command() {
  $items['user-blocker'] = array(
    'description' => 'Blocks user accounts with no activity in a
      period of time.',
    'aliases' => array('ub'),
    'examples' => array(
      'drush user-blocker' => 'Blocks user accounts who did not
        log in in the last two years.',
      'drush user-blocker en es' =>
```

```
            'Blocks user accounts who did not log in in the last two years
             whose default language is English or Spanish.',
           'drush user-blocker --since="two months ago" es' =>
             'Blocks user accounts which have Spanish as their default
             language and an account age ' .'
             of more than two months without activity.',
       ),
       'bootstrap' => DRUSH_BOOTSTRAP_DRUPAL_FULL,
       'arguments' => array(
         'languages' => 'A list of languages to filter user accounts.',
       ),
       'options' => array(
         'since' =>
           'Specifies last time a user account should have logged in ' .
           'so it won't get blocked. Defaults to 2 years ago. Accepts ' .
           'all date formats described at ' .
           'http://www.php.net/manual/en/dtetime.formats.php.show.',
       ),
   );
   return $items;
}
```

The second part implements the command callback. It first gathers arguments and options and then performs the SQL query to block users:

```
/**
 * Callback implementation for user-blocker command
 */
function drush_user_blocker() {
  // Grab all languages given. If any.
  $languages = func_get_args();
  // See if we received a date from which we should filter
  $since = strtotime(drush_get_option('since', '2 years ago'));
  // Perform the update over the users table
  $query= db_update('users')
  ->fields(array('status' => 0,))
  ->condition('uid', array(0, 1), 'NOT IN')
  ->condition('access', array(1, $since), 'BETWEEN');
  // Add the condition to filter by language
  if (count($languages)) {
    $query->condition('language', $languages, 'IN');
  }
```

```
$total_blocked = $query->execute();
drush_log(dt("Blocked !total_blocked users", array('!total_blocked'
=> $total_blocked)), 'success');
}
```

Save the file. Let's verify that the command was loaded by reading its help information in the main Drush help:

```
$ drush help
...
Other commands: (userblocker)
user-blocker (ub)      Blocks user accounts with no activity
```

Our command is listed at the end of the output. This is fine for just one command, but if you define many commands and they do not fit in any of the existing categories, you can classify it within the drush help output by implementing hook_drush_help(). More information about this hook can be seen by executing drush topic docs-examplecommand. Now let's see the detailed description of our command:

```
$ drush help user-blocker
Blocks user accounts with no activity
Examples:
drush user-blocker            Blocks user accounts who did not log in in
                              the last two years.

drush user-blocker en es      Blocks user accounts who did not log in in
                              the last two years and whose default
                              language is English or Spanish.

drush user-blocker            Blocks user accounts which have Spanish
--since="two months ago" es   as their
                              default language and an account age of
                              more than two months without activity.
Arguments:
roles of roles. Note that you have to wrap a role between quotes if
it has a space in its name.
Options:
--since Specifies the date that marks the last time a user account should
have logged in so it wont get blocked. Defaults to 2 years ago. Accepts
all date formats described at http://www.php.net/manual/en/
datetime.formats.php.show.
Aliases: ub
```

The previous information is extracted from the first hook implemented at the command file: hook_drush_command(). It shows its basic description, examples, arguments, options, and command aliases.

When writing commands, keep an eye at the **Drush API** as it describes a lot of functions that will be very useful for your scripts http://api.drush.org/api/functions.

Following is how we can quickly test our command before studying its implementation:

```
$ drush user-create user1
$ drush sql-query "update {users} set access=1 where name = 'user1';"
$ drush user-blocker
Blocked 1 users.
```

> Several date fields in Drupal such as the created, access, and login fields in the users table are stored as **Unix Timestamps**. A Unix Timestamp represents time through the number of seconds since 1st of January, 1970. This means that if we set the age of a user account to 1, it means *one second after the first of January of 1970*.

Analyzing the definition of our command

Now we are going to analyze the source code of our command to understand how it works and then improve it.

The first function defined contains the implementation of hook_drush_command(). This hook is used to tell Drush about commands implemented in the file. They are defined as a keyed array; the key of each element being the command name. Following is a description of each of the properties defined within the key user-blocker:

- description: This is used to describe our command when drush help is executed and at the top of the description when drush help user-blocker is executed.

- aliases: This is an array with a list of shortcuts for our command.

- examples: This is an array with pairs of command => expected result examples given. You should try to cover the most illustrative cases as it will help users to understand what your command is capable of.

- arguments: This is an array with each argument name and its description. Single valued arguments (such as integers or strings) are normally defined here and then received in the callback function as variables. Variable length arguments (such as in our command) are obtained in the callback function through func_get_args() as an array.

- `options`: This is an array with a list of options that our command accepts and their respective descriptions. Options can be accessed within the callback function using `drush_get_option('option name', 'default value')`.

There are other important options not defined in our command, such as:

- `callback`: This is the function that will be called to process different commands. If not defined, Drush looks for a function with the structure `drush_COMMANDFILE_commandname()` with underscores instead of dashes. If you choose to define a callback, it must start with `drush_COMMANDFILE_` (for example, `drush_user_blocker_block`). It is recommended to omit this option.

- `bootstrap`: This defines up to which level a Drupal site should be bootstrapped. Defaults to `DRUSH_BOOTSTRAP_DRUPAL_FULL`, which does a full Drupal bootstrap similar to when we open a site in a web server. There are several levels of bootstrapping such as `DRUSH_BOOTSTRAP_DRUSH`, which is used by commands that do not need a Drupal directory to be executed. Read the contents of `drush topic bootstrap` for detailed information about other levels.

- `core`: If this command has limited version support, specify it here. Examples of this are 6, 7 or 6+.

- `drupal dependencies` and `drush dependencies`: Drupal modules or Drush command files that this command may require, respectively.

Analyzing the implementation of our command

After a quick look at the code of our callback function, we can see that apart from `drush_get_option()` and `drush_print()` the rest is day-to-day Drupal code. This is good news because it means that we can use the **Drupal API**s within our command when a Drupal site is bootstrapped. So far, the code is very simple and it just grabs the list of languages, calculates the date of the last time a user must have logged in, and finally performs a SQL query to block user accounts, which match the criteria. Let's set a user with Spanish as default language; an old last access date and then test our command again:

```
$ drush sql-query "update {users} set status=1, access=1, \
  language='es' where name = 'user1';"

$ drush user-blocker es

Blocked 1 users.
```

The previous command blocked one user account that also matched to Spanish as its default language. Languages are grabbed in the command at the following lines as an array and then added to the SQL query:

```
// Grab all languages given
$languages = func_get_args();
```

Drush provides the command `drush_get_option()` to catch options if they are given. Let's first see a working example and then examine the code. We will set the last access date of our test user account to one hour ago and run the command again:

```
$ drush sql-query "update {users} set status=1, \
   access=(unix_timestamp() - 3600) where name = 'user1';"
$ drush user-blocker --since="1 hour ago" es
Blocked 1 users.
```

The previous command blocked the account as we changed the default last access date from two hours to one with the `--since` option.

Options and arguments can be used together as we saw in *Chapter 1, Installation and Basic Usage*. Following is a command example of how we could block user accounts, which last accessed the site more than a year ago, and have Spanish, English, or French as their default language. We will also use the command alias that we defined:

```
$ drush ub --since="1 year ago" es en fr
```

As you can see, options and arguments provide higher flexibility so our commands can cover the widest range of scenarios. In the next section, we will validate them.

Validating input

We are assuming that all the arguments and options given through the command line are safe and valid, but in order to make our command robust we have to validate the input. We will implement `drush_hook_COMMAND_validate()` to add some logic that ensures that the options and arguments given are valid. Add the following code below `userblocker_drush_command()` in the file `userblocker.drush.inc`:

```
/**
 * Implementation of drush_hook_COMMAND_validate()
 */
function drush_userblocker_user_blocker_validate() {
  // Validates language arguments if they were given
  $languages = func_get_args();
  if (count($languages)) {
```

```
      $languages = array_unique($languages);
      $valid_languages = array_intersect(
        $languages, array_keys(language_list()));
      if (count($languages) != count($valid_languages)) {
        return drush_set_error('INVALID_LANGUAGE', dt(
          'At least one of the languages given does not exist.'));
      }
    }
    // Validates if a valid date was given
    if (drush_get_option('since')) {
      if (!strtotime(drush_get_option('since'))) {
        return drush_set_error('INVALID_SINCE_DATE', dt(
          'The date given as --since option is invalid.'));
      }
    }
  }
}
```

The previous code validates the languages and date given. Note that the function name follows the format that we explained before: **hook** is the name of our command file (userblocker), and **COMMAND** is the name of our command using underscores instead of dashes (user_blocker). We added some logic to make sure that all languages provided exist in our site (in case the user misspelled one of them) and that the date provided in the --since option is a valid date that can be converted to a timestamp through strtotime(). If any of this validations failed then we set an error by calling to drush_set_error(), which will stop the execution and print a message. Drush can translate strings (such as the error descriptions) using the function dt(), which is a wrapper for the well know t() function from Drupal. Now we will test our command to verify that it validates user input:

```
$ drush user-blocker --since="nonsense date"
The date given as --since option is invalid [error]
$ drush user-blocker en es
At least one of the languages given do not exist [error]
$ drush user-blocker --since="1970" en
Blocked 0 users [success]
```

First, we executed the command with a string date that cannot be converted to a timestamp, hence we did not pass validation. Then we attempted to block user accounts with English and Spanish as their default languages, but the fact is that Spanish language has not been enabled nor the Locale module so again an error was reported. We finally verified that the command works as expected by giving it a valid language and a valid date, which returned a **success** message although we did not block any user account.

Altering and reacting to existing commands

Drush offers a very broad list of hooks to interact with existing commands. We can modify, react and extend them however we need it. We are going to demonstrate this by first describing each hook and then writing and testing an example that uses some of them. Following is the full list of hooks sorted by the order in which they are called with a short description of each one:

- `hook_drush_init()` is executed before any command is run.
- `drush_COMMAND_init()` is called before a command is validated.
- `drush_hook_COMMAND_validate()` validates a command. We used it in our custom command example in the previous section (`drush_userblocker_user_blocker_validate()`).
- `drush_hook_pre_COMMAND()` operates before a command is going to be executed.
- `drush_hook_COMMAND()` is the default callback implementation of a defined command at `hook_drush_command()`.
- `drush_hook_post_COMMAND()` runs after a command has been executed.
- `hook_drush_exit()` is called after any command is run.

Whenever any of the previous hooks report an error by using `drush_set_error()` or by returning FALSE, the normal execution stops and the **rollback mechanism** starts by calling the respective rollback hooks backwards in time. This means, for example, if an error is reported at `drush_hook_post_COMMAND()`, then the implemented rollback functions will be called in the following order:

1. `drush_hook_COMMAND_rollback()`
2. `drush_hook_pre_COMMAND_rollback()`
3. `drush_hook_COMMAND_validate_rollback()`
4. `drush_hook_post_COMMAND_rollback()`

The rollback mechanism helps you to keep your system in a consistent status when an error is reported. If you are doing a long process within a command that needs a rollback mechanism, use the previously given hooks to implement the logic needed. To see which rollback functions are available for a command, execute it with the option `--show-invoke`.

You can find more hooks and examples by typing drush `topic docs-api` in the command line.

Altering an existing command

Now we will go through a practical example. We are going to create a new Drush command file located at the `.drush` folder of our home directory which will enable downloaded projects, when the option `--enable` is given. Create a file named `autoenable.drush.inc` and place it in `$HOME/.drush/autoenable.drush.inc` with the following contents:

```php
<?php
/**
 * @file
 * Enables modules after they have been downloaded
 */
/**
 * Implementation of hook_drush_help_alter()
 * Adds an option "enable" to pm-download command.
 */
function autoenable_drush_help_alter(&$command) {
  if ($command['command'] == 'pm-download') {
    $command['options']['enable'] = "Enable the module
automatically.";
  }
}
/**
 * Implementation of drush_hook_post_COMMAND()
 * Hooks into pm-download when it has finished an enables the module
automatically.
 */
function autoenable_drush_pm_post_download($request, $release) {
  $phase = drush_get_context('DRUSH_BOOTSTRAP_PHASE');
  if (($phase >= DRUSH_BOOTSTRAP_DRUPAL_SITE) &&
      drush_get_option('enable')) {
    if (file_exists($request['full_project_path'] .
      DIRECTORY_SEPARATOR .
      $request['name'] . '.info')) {
      drush_invoke('pm-enable', $request['name']);
    }
  }
}
```

The previous command, being in our `.drush` directory, is available for all our Drupal sites. Before diving into its logic, let's run a few commands to see what it does. First of all, we have added an option to the `pm-download` command called `--enable`. It is now visible in the help information of the command:

```
$ drush help pm-download
```

...

```
Options:
```

`--destination`	`Path to which the project will be copied. If you're providing a relative path, note it is relative to the drupal root (if bootstrapped).`
`--enable`	`Enable the module automatically.`

```
Aliases: dl
```

The previous option was added by the first function defined in our file, which is an implementation of `hook_drush_help_alter()`. This hook allows us to modify the properties of an existing command.

Now we are going to test the second function, an implementation of `drush_hook_post_COMMAND()`, which performs an operation once a command has completed its execution (in this case, a module has been downloaded within a Drupal site). We will download the Token module and add the option `--enable` so it gets enabled automatically without having to call `pm-enable` afterwards. We will also add the option `--yes` so we do not have to answer to the prompt confirming the act of enabling the module:

```
$ cd /home/juampy/drupal
$ drush pm-download --enable --yes token
Project token (7.x-1.0-beta7) downloaded to /home/juampy/projects/drupal/
sites/all/modules/contrib/token.  [success]
The following extensions will be enabled: token
Do you really want to continue? (y/n): y
token was enabled successfully. [ok]
```

That's it. The `pm-download` command placed Token module at `sites/all/modules/contrib/token`. Once it finished, `drush_hook_post_pm_download()` was invoked so our hook implementation was called, thus enabling the module.

If you see the source code of `autoenable_drush_pm_post_download()`, you will notice there are two conditions that must be met in order for the module to be enabled: we must be within a Drupal site and the enable option must have been given when `pm-download` was executed. These two requirements are checked at:

```
$phase = drush_get_context('DRUSH_BOOTSTRAP_PHASE');

if (($phase >= DRUSH_BOOTSTRAP_DRUPAL_SITE) &&
  drush_get_option('enable')) {
```

After that, the function evaluates if the module was downloaded successfully and there is a `token.info` file within the module (unfortunately not all modules follow this convention). If it does, we make use of the function `drush_invoke()` to call the `pm-enable` command with the project name as an argument, which is done at the following line:

```
drush_invoke('pm-enable', $request['name']);
```

The previous code was just an example of how you can alter existing commands. Now go on and start thinking about how you can extend commands to make your day to day work easier by implementing a few of these hooks.

Executing custom PHP scripts

Sometimes you may only need to run a few PHP commands after bootstrapping Drupal. For example, to view the value of a server variable, to programmatically submit a form, and to print the output of a very complex database query that needs some placeholders. Normally, to achieve this, you would copy `index.php` to a temporary file, remove the line that invokes the controller and type in your own code. Drush helps you do this more easily and securely through the commands `php-eval` and `php-script`.

Executing PHP code from the command line

`php-eval` accepts some PHP code between quotes and executes it. If it can bootstrap a Drupal site, it will do it first, allowing us to interact with it. Here are a couple of examples:

```
$ cd /home/juampy/projects
$ drush php-eval "print ini_get('error_reporting');"
30719
$ drush php-eval "print variable_get('site_name', 'not found');"
PHP Fatal error:  Call to undefined function variable_get() in
  /usr/share/drush/commands/core/core.drush.inc(637) :
  eval()'d code on line 1
Drush command terminated abnormally due to an unrecoverable error.
                                                          [error]
```

```
$ cd drupal
$ ls sites/
all   default   example.sites.php
$ drush php-eval "print variable_get('site_name', 'not found');"
Festival
```

We firstly placed ourselves at a non Drupal directory and executed a couple of commands. The first one worked fine as it was pure PHP code, but the second one failed because Drush could not bootstrap a Drupal site. After that, we changed directory to the root of a Drupal site with its `settings.php` located at `sites/default` (which is discoverable by Drush) and executed the same command. Drush found the `settings.php`, bootstrapped Drupal, and extracted the value from the variables table.

 You can execute several PHP statements by separating them with semicolons.

Executing PHP scripts

Evaluating PHP code from the command line is fine with two or three PHP statements. More than that becomes harder to read and tricky to escape if it has double or single quotes. This is when we'd rather use a PHP script that the `php-script` command will execute for us after bootstrapping Drupal.

If you need to keep these scripts, it is a good practice to keep them outside your Drupal installation or in a safe directory within Drupal so they won't get executed in a production environment by mistake.

Let's suppose that we want to delete all comments submitted by a particular user. We could create the following script to accomplish it. Create a file named `delete-comments.php` outside of your Drupal root path with the following contents:

```php
<?php
// Custom PHP script to delete comments made by a user id
$uid = 100; // The user id (uid). Set this to the uid of the user
whose comments you want to delete.
$result = db_select('comment', 'c')
  ->fields('c', array('cid'))
  ->condition('uid', $uid)
  ->execute();
$counter = 0;
foreach ($result as $record) {
```

```
    comment_delete($record['cid']);
    $counter++;
}
print "Deleted " . $counter . " comments.";
```

Now we will change directory to the Drupal root where we want to execute and run it:

```
$ cd /home/juampy/projects/drupal
$ drush php-script --script-path=../ delete-comments
Deleted 72 comments.
```

We specified the path where the script is (one level higher for this example) and the filename without the extension (our filename is `delete-comments.php`, so we only have to type `delete-comments`). Then Drush bootstrapped Drupal and executed our script.

You can list all scripts available from your current path and by paths provided by the `--script-path` option by not typing a script filename, like in the following example:

```
$ drush php-script –script-path=../
/usr/share/drush/commands/core/scratch.php
/home/juampy/projects/drupal/authorize.php
/home/juampy/projects/drupal/install.php
/home/juampy/projects/drupal/xmlrpc.php
/home/juampy/projects/drupal/update.php
/home/juampy/projects/drupal/cron.php
/home/juampy/projects/drupal/index.php
../delete-comments.php
```

Type less and do more with Drush Site Aliases

At this point in the book, you may have already executed quite a few commands. Some of them need a long list of attributes and options in order to behave as your needs demand. Plus, you always have to take care of being at the root of your Drupal site. Moreover, if you use named sites in your `sites` folder instead of using the `sites/default` directory, you always have to add the `--uri` option or execute commands from the `settings.php` path. This is annoying and makes command typing tiresome and prone to error.

Enter Drush Site Aliases. A site alias is a short name that defines several options about a local or remote Drupal site such as where it is located, what is the username, host to log in via SSH, which sites has it defined at its sites directory, and many more. Think of it as an array with options.

We will first explain what are the benefits of setting up **local site aliases**, and then go one step further and start invoking Drush commands to Drupal sites located in other systems through **remote site aliases**.

Configuring a Local Alias

We will start by defining a site alias for our Drupal testing site and try a few commands with it. Create the file `drupal.alias.drushrc.php` within your `.drush` directory with the following contents:

```php
<?php
/**
 * @file
 * Site alias for local site called "Drupal"
 */
$aliases['drupal'] = array(
  // Set here the path to the root of your Drupal installation.
  'root' => '/home/juampy/projects/drupal/',
  // Here goes the URL of your site.
  'uri'  => 'drupal.localhost',
);
```

As you can see in the previous given code, we are defining an array `$aliases` (respect this variable name so Drush can discover the alias) that defines a site alias called `drupal` with the following options:

- `root`: the root path of our Drupal site.
- `uri`: the URL of our site. This will be used as a `--uri` option with each command being executed.

Now let's see how to use our brand new site alias with some Drush commands:

```
$ drush site-alias
@drupal
$ drush @drupal status
 Drupal version        :  7.10
 Site URI              :  drupal.localhost
 Database driver       :  mysql
```

```
Database hostname        :   localhost
Database username        :   root
Database name            :   drupal
Database                 :   Connected
Drupal bootstrap         :   Successful
Drupal user              :   Anonymous
Default theme            :   bartik
Administration theme     :   seven
PHP configuration        :   /etc/php5/apache2/php.ini
Drush version            :   4.5
Drush configuration      :
Drush alias files        :   /home/juampy/.drush/drupal.alias.drushrc.php
Drupal root              :   /home/juampy/projects/drupal/
Site path                :   sites/default
File directory path      :   sites/default/files
```

We first executed the `site-alias` command to list our configured aliases, from which we could verify that Drush discovered our site alias. Then we checked the status of our test Drupal site by running `drush @drupal status`. If you remember **Telling Drush Which Site to Work With in** *Chapter 1*, *Installation and Basic Usage* there were two ways of executing a command for a particular site:

1. Going to the directory where the `settings.php` is and run the command there unless `settings.php` is at `sites/default`, in which case we can run it from the root path:

    ```
    $ cd /home/juampy/projects/drupal/sites/drupal.localhost
    $ drush cache-clear all
    'all' cache was [success]
    ```

2. Adding the `--root` and `--uri` as options when executing the command from any directory in our system:

    ```
    $ drush --root=/home/juampy/projects/drupal –uri=drupal.localhost
        cache-clear all
    'all' cache was [success]
    ```

Now with our Drush site alias we can execute commands about our site by just adding `@drupal` before the command name, such as the following:

```
$ drush @drupal cc all
'all' cache was was cleared              [success]
```

The previous command is actually reading the options defined at the array located at $HOME/drush/drupal.alias.drushrc.php and adding them to the command. This is why it can find it and execute it successfully.

 Executing drush --full --with-optional site-alias @ self >> ~/.drush/mysite.alias.drushrc.php from a site within the sites directory will print a basic alias array into a site alias file. This is a very useful way to start configuring site aliases.

Organizing Site Aliases within our system

As you may have noticed, defining site aliases for our local sites is an efficient way of shortening frequently used commands. We may have many sites and therefore end up with many site aliases. Hence, it is good to know how best to organize them.

Site aliases will be scanned and loaded from the following locations and in this order (paraphrased from drush topic docs-aliases):

1. If you define a drushrc.php configuration file at the root of your site, Drush will inspect it to see if $options['alias-path'] is defined and look for site aliases there. You can also set this by adding the option --alias-path in the command line. Further info about this on **Using Configuration Files** is at the end of this chapter.

2. Any of the following locations:

    ° $ETC_PREFIX/etc/drush, where $ETC_PREFIX is an environment variable.

    ° In the directory where Drush has been installed. For example, at /usr/share/drush.

    ° Inside the aliases folder where Drush has been installed, such as /usr/share/drush/aliases.

    ° At the .drush directory located at your home path. This is the recommended location.

3. Inside the sites folder of any loaded Drupal site.

There are three ways of defining site aliases in files:

• Single site aliases that reference one site can be placed each in a separate file called ALIASNAME.alias.drushrc.php, such as the file we created in the previous section with the filename drupal.alias.drushrc.php.

- Different site aliases from different and non related sites can be placed together in a single file called `aliases.drushrc.php`. Here is an example of how could we remove `drupal.alias.drushrc.php` and define it next to other site aliases at `$HOME/.drush/aliases.drushrc.php`:

```php
<?php
/**
 * @file
 * Definition of several site aliases
 */
$aliases['drupal'] = array(
  'root' => '/home/juampy/projects/drupal/',
  'uri'  => 'drupal.localhost',
);
$aliases['drupal8'] = array(
  'root' => '/home/juampy/projects/drupal8/',
  'uri'  => 'drupal8.localhost',
);
$aliases['anothersite'] = array(
...
```

- A group of related site aliases can be put together at a file called `GROUPNAME.aliases.drushrc.php`. This gives some extra benefits such as inheriting properties from other site aliases and namespacing site aliases in the form of `@GROUPNAME.alias` when using them in the command line. This format comes in handy when defining site aliases for local, development and production sites, where they may be located in different systems but refer to different instances of the same website. We will go over its details in the next section through a practical example.

Interacting with remote sites

A very common scenario in the development process of a Drupal site is having a local copy of the site in our local system, another in a development server, and a third one in the production server. Remote site aliases make interactions between these three incredibly easy and give us the chance to invoke commands against the remote sites without even having to login there first. However, dealing with remote sites requires that we have previously established password-less authentication with each server through **SSH** and a **Public Key**.

If you already have SSH access to a remote server where a Drupal site is installed, you can set up password-less access in Linux and Mac with the following steps. Instructions for setting up password-less SSH access in Windows can be found at `http://drupal.org/node/1418122`.

1. Generate a public key for your user if you do not have one already with the following command. Execute the following command and hit *Enter* on every prompt:

    ```
    $ ssh-keygen
    ```

2. Copy your public key to the remote server. Replace **username** and **hostname** in the command by your SSH username and server domain or IP address. Enter the password of your SSH account when asked:

    ```
    $ ssh-copy-id username@hostname
    ```

    ```
    username@hostname's password:
    ```

    ```
    Now try logging into the machine, with "ssh 'username@hostname'",
    and check in: ~/.ssh/authorized_keys
    ```

    ```
    to make sure we haven't added extra keys that you weren't
    expecting.
    ```

3. Our key has been added and now we do not need to enter a password to identify ourselves. Try to login into the server:

    ```
    $ ssh username@hostname
    ```

    ```
    Welcome!
    ```

 If you have any trouble setting up password-less SSH authentication, you can find plenty of debugging information at `http://drupal.org/node/670460`.

Grouping related Site Aliases

Let's suppose that we maintain a website about a music festival (we will call it `http://festival.drush`). For this website we have a Drupal site configured at our local system, a development environment in another system, and the production environment in a third one. We have already tested that we can access the development and production systems through SSH without typing a password. If you have a similar scenario or can set up one for testing, you will be able to customize the following examples to fit your scenario. If you do so, it is recommended to add the `--simulate` option to your commands in order to avoid unexpected results.

Creating a Grouped Alias file with our Local Site Alias

In the previous section, we said that we could group related site aliases together in a single file named with the GROUPNAME.aliases.drushrc.php format. Therefore, we are going to create a file named festival.aliases.drushrc.php at our .drush folder located in our home directory with the site alias definition of our local copy of Festival:

```php
<?php
/**
 * @file
 * Site aliases for Festival website
 */
/**
 * Local site alias (http://festival.localhost)
 */
$aliases['local'] = array(
  'root' => '/home/juampy/projects/festival',
  'uri'  => 'festival.localhost',
);
```

The previous site alias looks exactly the same as the ones we have previously defined apart from the highlighted line, but the first difference we will encounter by placing it within a file with the filename GROUPNAME.aliases.drushrc.php is visible when we list the available site aliases:

```
$ drush site-alias

@festival.local
```

In the previous site alias that we defined, the array index at $alias was then the resulting @alias that we would use later in our commands, however, in a grouped site alias, the group name prefixes our site alias name (that is why it is @festival.local and not @local). For example, if we wanted to clear the cache we would use the following syntax:

```
$ drush @festival.local cache-clear all

'all' cache was cleared       [success]
```

Adding a Site Alias for the development site

Now we are going to add another site alias that will connect us with the copy of Festival in the development server. Add the following at the end of `festival.aliases.drushrc.php`:

```
/**
 * Development site alias (http://festival.dev.drush)
 */
$aliases['dev'] = array (
  'uri' => 'festival.dev.drush',
  'root' => '/var/www/festival.dev.drush',
  'remote-user' => 'username',
  'remote-host' => 'festival.dev.drush',
);
```

Now our site alias file for Festival has two site aliases: one for our local site and one for the development site. We have added two new properties there that define the username and hostname used for the SSH connection (this means that the connection command used internally will be `ssh username@festival.dev.drush`). You should replace these two by the username and hostname of the remote system that you want to connect to. The **uri** and **root** options define properties about the Drupal site installed in that server.

If we now list the available site aliases, we will see how the namespacing property of grouped site aliases makes the resulting site alias names meaningful:

```
$ drush site-alias
@festival.local
@festival.dev
```

In the previous output, we can see that our site aliases for Festival are prefixed by the GROUPNAME defined in the alias filename, and the rest is the index that we defined in the $alias array. Now you should verify that the new site alias is correctly configured by obtaining information about the remote site:

```
$ drush @festival.dev core-status
Drupal version         :  7.10
Site URI               :  festival.dev.drush
Database driver        :  mysql
Database hostname      :  localhost
Database username      :  festivaldevdrush
Database name          :  festivaldevdrush
```

```
Database                  :  Connected

Drupal bootstrap          :  Successful

Drupal user               :  Anonymous

Default theme             :  bartik

Administration theme      :  seven

PHP configuration         :  /etc/php5/cli/php.ini

Drush version             :  4.5

Drush configuration       :

Drush alias files         :

Drupal root               :  /var/www/festival.dev.drush

Site path                 :  sites/festival.dev.drush

File directory path       :  sites/festival.dev.drush/files

Private file  directory path  :  sites/festival.dev.drush/private/files
```

If you got an output similar to the previous one, you have successfully configured your remote site alias. Now you can make use of all the commands we have already explained against this Drupal site without having to login into the remote system. Go ahead and try some commands to see how this could help you in other projects.

Things we can do with remote Site Aliases

So far we have our remote site alias working and we can do a lot with it, but the real power of remote site aliases comes when we synchronize a local site with a remote site or vice versa. Synchronizing helps us automate the following scenarios:

- Extract a MySQL dump of a remote site, download it, and load it into the database of our local copy of the site. This is done with the sql-sync command.

- Copy the directory structure (or any subdirectory) from a remote site into our local site. This is done by the core-rsync command and it is useful for downloading the contents of the files directory.

- Assuming that our local and development sites are working, we will start by configuring our site aliases in order to synchronize databases between them.

 If you have problems setting up site aliases or testing the commands listed in the following sections, add the option --verbose to the command and try to debug what is going wrong by reading the extra output that this option produces.

Synchronizing databases

We are going to add some options to our @festival.local and @festival.dev
site aliases so we can synchronize their databases. We basically need to add a path
to store temporary database dumps generated on the execution of the sql-sync
command and some extra performance options.

Update the file festival.aliases.drushrc.php with the following highlighted
pieces of code:

```php
<?php
/**
 * @file
 * Site aliases for Festival website
 */
/**
 * Local alias (http://festival.localhost)
 */
$aliases['local'] = array(
 root' => '/home/juampy/projects/festival',
  'uri'  => 'festival.localhost',
  'path-aliases' => array(
    '%dump-dir' => '/tmp',
  ),
);
/**
 * Development alias (http://festival.dev.drush)
 */
$aliases['dev'] = array (
  'uri' => 'festival.dev.drush',
  'root' => '/var/www/festival.dev.drush',
  'remote-user' => 'username',
  'remote-host' => 'festival.dev.drush',
  'path-aliases' => array(
    '%dump-dir' => '/tmp',
  ),
  'source-command-specific' => array(
    'sql-sync' => array(
      'no-cache' => TRUE,
      'structure-tables-key' => 'common',
    ),
  ),
  'command-specific' => array(
```

```
    'sql-sync' => array (
      'no-ordered-dump' => TRUE,
      'sanitize' => TRUE,
      'structure-tables' => array(
        'common' => array('cache', 'cache_filter', 'cache_menu',
                    'cache_page', 'history', 'sessions', 'watchdog'),
      ),
    ),
  ),
);
```

We have added one option to our local site alias (@festival.local) and two to the remote one (@festival.dev). Following is a description of each of them:

- **path-aliases** (present in both site aliases) is an array of variables used by some commands. The help information of the sql-sync command suggests that we define a temporary path in both site aliases (the one that will generate the database dump and the one which will receive it) for storing the MySQL dump files. Alternatively, this can be provided by appending the --source-dump and --target-dump options when executing sql-sync in the command line.

- **source-command-specific** defines a few properties for the site alias used as a source for the sql-command. In this case, we do not want to cache database dumps, which means that a database dump is generated every time we call the command, and we are also stating that we want to ignore the data of a set of tables defined in the next option. These two options could be given at run time by appending --no-cache and --structure-tables-key=common in the command line.

- **command-specific** sets a few options for the sql-dump command. This is the same as adding --sanitize and --no-ordered-dump in the command line when sql-sync is executed. Here is the meaning of each one:
  - sanitize resets automatically user email addresses to user+%uid@localhost and passwords to password.
  - Options such as --sanitize-passwords and --sanitize-email can also be used to specify how these two should be sanitized.
  - no-ordered-dump avoids the database entries to be sorted, which speeds up the process.
  - structure-tables defines the an array with table names whose data should not be extracted (for example, the cache tables).

You can set specific settings for the source site alias and the target site alias by using the options `--source-command-specific` and `--target-command-specific`. Read the contents of `drush topic docs-aliases` for more information.

Now let's test our command and synchronize the remote database with our local one. Depending on the size of the remote database and the available bandwidth this could take some time to complete. It is important to provide the site alias names in the right order for this command to work as expected. The first one is the source site alias **from** which the data will be extracted, and the second one is the target site alias **to** receive the data:

```
$ drush sql-sync @festival.dev @festival.local
The following tables will be skipped:
  cache, cache_filter, cache_menu, cache_page, history, sessions,
watchdog
You will destroy data from festival and replace with data from festival.
dev.org/festival.dev.org.
WARNING: --sanitize was specified, but deferred (e.g. the source site
is remote).  The sanitization operations will be determined after the
database is copied to the local system and will be run without further
confirmation.  Run with --confirm-sanitizations to force confirmation
after the sync.
You might want to make a backup first, using the sql-dump command.
Do you really want to continue? (y/n): y
The following post-sync operations will be done on the destination:
  * Reset passwords and email addresses in user table
```

If you got an output such as the previous one, you successfully synchronized the remote database with your local one. As you can see in the output, the list of tables we specified was skipped (their data was not extracted) and after the database dump was loaded in our local system the sanitization process started. Now you have a copy of the remote database in your local host. If you wanted to synchronize your local database with the remote database, you could run the following command:

```
$  drush sql-sync @festival.local @festival.dev \
  --structure-tables-key=common --no-ordered-dump \
  --sanitize=0 --no-cache
```

 In order to set up security rules that avoid someone from accidentally upload his local database to the remote site, read the contents of `drush topic docs-policy`.

Synchronizing directories

There will be times when we need to obtain source code from a remote site to our local copy. The command `core-rsync` copies a full Drupal directory tree between sites identified by site aliases.

In its simplest form, we just need to define the source site alias and the destination site alias, like we did for the `sql-sync` command. In the following example, we are downloading all source code and files from the remote site (http://festival.dev. drush) to our local one (http://festival.localhost):

```
$ drush core-rsync @festival.dev @festival.local
You will destroy data from /home/juampy/projects/festival/ and replace
with data from username@hostname:/var/www/festival/
Do you really want to continue? (y/n): y
```

It is good practice to read the confirmation message where the source site alias and the target site alias located in the synchronization. If you need to do this frequently, it is an even better practice to pull code via **Git** rather than using `drush rsync`.

When we execute the command we can specify paths next to each site alias. Placeholders can be defined at the `path-aliases` option within the site alias definition. Drush adds one for us automatically for handling the `files` directory of a site. This means that we can easily synchronize our `files` directory with the folder in the remote site with the following command:

```
$ drush core-rsync @festival.dev:%files @festival.local:%files
```

 For more options and specific synchronizations, read the available help information at `drush help core-rsync`.

Sharing configuration within Grouped Aliases

We are about to add a third alias to our group aliases file that will represent the production environment of the Festival website. The most logical step would be to open `festival.aliases.drushrc.php` and copy the array that defines the development environment to a new entry called `prod` and edit each of its options. However, we are going to make use of the `parent` option within the site alias definition to reuse the configuration of the development alias.

The following is how our `festival.aliases.drushrc.php` looks after adding the new site alias. Note that if you are following this with your own production site, you will have to alter each setting so it fits your scenario:

```php
<?php
/**
 * @file
 * Site aliases for Festival website
 */
/**
 * Local site alias (http://festival.localhost)
 */
$aliases['local'] = array(
  'root' => '/home/juampy/projects/festival',
  'uri'  => 'festival.localhost',
  'path-aliases' => array(
    '%dump-dir' => '/tmp',
  ),
);
/**
 * Development site alias (http://festival.dev.drush)
 */
$aliases['dev'] = array (
  'uri' => 'festival.dev.drush',
  'root' => '/var/www/festival.dev.drush',
  'remote-user' => 'username',
  'remote-host' => 'festival.dev.drush',
  'path-aliases' => array(
    '%dump-dir' => '/tmp',
  ),
  'source-command-specific' => array(
    'sql-sync' => array(
      'no-cache' => TRUE,
      'structure-tables-key' => 'common',
    ),
  ),
  'command-specific' => array(
    'sql-sync' => array (
      'no-ordered-dump' => TRUE,
      'sanitize' => TRUE,
      'structure-tables' => array(
        'common' => array('cache', 'cache_filter', 'cache_menu',
        'cache_page', 'history','sessions', 'watchdog'),
      ),
```

```
      ),
     ),
  );
  /**
   * Production site alias (http://festival.drush)
   */
  $aliases['prod'] = array (
    'parent' => '@festival.dev',
    'uri' => 'festival.drush',
    'root' => '/var/www/festival.drush',
    'remote-user' => 'username-prod',
    'remote-host' => 'festival.drush',
  );
```

The option **'parent' => '@festival.dev'** is telling Drush that we are inheriting all the options defined at the **$aliases['dev']** array. This means that we can just focus on defining what is different in this site alias, which are options such as the **uri** and **root** path, the connection parameters (**remote-user** and **remote-host**), and the location of the **files** directory.

After doing this, we finally have a structure of three namespaced site alias like the following example:

```
$ drush site-alias

@festival.local

@festival.dev

@festival.prod
```

As you can see, there is an alias defined for each environment and we could copy the `festival.aliases.drushrc.php` file to other systems and use it by just adapting the local site alias. Now we can download a sanitized version of the production system to our local system with the following command:

```
$ drush sql-sync @festival.prod @festival.local
```

The output must have been almost identical to the development system. Drush detected that we want to sanitize the database (it actually loaded this option from the inherited alias `@festival.dev`) and decided to postpone it until the database dump had been loaded to our local Drupal site.

> If you are not sure about what would be the result `sql-sync` or a `core-rsync` command, you can always simulate it by adding the `--simulate` option at the command line.

Using configuration files

Drush lets us set up configuration files that modify how it works system-wide, user-wide, or site-wide. These files are named `drushrc.php` and contain a list of array options. With a configuration file, we can do things such as the following:

- Set the `--uri` and `--root` options to be added to every command that we execute from the root path of a multisite Drupal installation

- Automatically check for Drush updates

- Load additional site alias files located in a given directory

- Specify where to store database dumps, which tables to ignore completely, and which one's data to ignore

- Always display verbose information on each command

- Add options when a specific command is executed

- Override elements of the `variables` table of a site

Drush will look for configuration files in the following locations (extracted from `drush topic docs-configuration`):

- Next to a `settings.php` file of a Drupal site. For example, at `sites/default/drushrc.php` or `sites/drupal.localhost/drushrc.php`.

- The root directory of a Drupal installation. For example, at `/var/home/juampy/projects/drupal/drushrc.php`.

- When provided explicitly by adding the `--config` option in the command line, such as `drush --config=../drushrc.php core-status`.

- At the `.drush` folder located in the home path. For example, at `/var/home/juampy/.drush/drushrc.php`.

- At `/etc/drush/drushrc.php`, unless you have a prefix configured by the `ETC_PREFIX` setting at your `php.ini` file in which case it would be `ETC_PREFIX/etc/drush/drushrc.php`.

- At the Drush installation folder, such as at `/usr/share/drush/drushrc.php`.

Let's add a sample configuration file to our `.drush` directory and see how it affects the commands we execute. Create a `drushrc.php` file at the `.drush` folder of your home path, for example, at `/home/juampy/.drush/drushrc.php` with the following contents:

```
<?php
/**
 * Sample user wide configuration file for Drush
 */
```

```
// Activate verbose mode for all commands so they output extra
information.
$options['v'] = 1;
// Directory where database dumps generated by sql-dump will be stored
and format of the files.
$options['result-file'] = '/home/juampy/dbbackups/@DATABASE_@DATE.
sql';
// Print warning messages. This is a nice debugging measure when you
are writing a custom command.
$options['php-notices'] = 'warning';
// Generic list of tables whose data should be ignored on database
dumps
$options['structure-tables'] = array(
  'common' => array('cache', 'cache_filter', 'cache_menu', 'cache_
page', 'history', 'sessions', 'watchdog'),
);
```

We have activated the verbose mode for all commands (same as adding --verbose
in the command line); specified where to store database dump; added a debugging
option so PHP warnings will be printed; and defined a generic array of tables whose
data should be ignored on database synchronizations. Let's see how these options
affect to Drush's behavior:

```
$ mkdir ~/dbbackups

$ cd /home/juampy/projects/drupal

$ drush sql-dump

Initialized Drupal 7.10 root directory at /home/juampy/projects/drupal
[notice]

Initialized Drupal site default at sites/default   [notice]

Calling system(mysqldump --result-file
  /home/juampy/dbbackups/drupal_20120123_095735.sql --single-transaction
  --opt -Q  drupal --host=localhost --user=root --password= );

Database dump saved to /home/juampy/dbbackups/drupal_20120123_09573t.sql
[success]

Command dispatch complete [notice]
```

The output shows that **notice** messages are now displayed because of the verbose
mode being active and the directory for database dumps was being used. Extra info
is displayed such as the mysql command and the destination path of the backup is
the one we defined.

We also added a default array of tables to be ignored by Drush when sql-sync is
executed. From now on we could create site aliases that do not need to list the tables
to ignore unless it wants to modify the list.

The following is an example of how `festival.aliases.drushrc.php` would look like after adding that option to `drushrc.php`:

```php
<?php
/**
 * @file
 * Site aliases for Festival website
 */
...
/**
 * Development site alias (http://festival.dev.drush)
 */
$aliases['dev'] = array (
  'uri' => 'festival.dev.drush',
  'root' => '/var/www/festival.dev.drush',
  'remote-user' => 'username',
  'remote-host' => 'festival.dev.drush',
  'path-aliases' => array(
    '%dump-dir' => '/tmp',
  ),
  'source-command-specific' => array(
    'sql-sync' => array(
      'no-cache' => TRUE,
      'structure-tables-key' => 'common',
    ),
  ),
  'command-specific' => array(
    'sql-sync' => array (
      'no-ordered-dump' => TRUE,
      'sanitize' => TRUE,
      'structure-tables' => array{
          'common' => array('cache', 'cache_filter', 'cache_menu',
'cache_page', 'history',
                                    'sessions', 'watchdog'),
      ),
    ),
  ),
);
```

We have removed the `structure-tables` array from the site alias definition because it will be taken from the `drushrc.php` file. You could apply this to other options and thus make your site aliases shorter. However, there are modules that define additional cache tables, in which case you should redefine here the array includes them.

Optimizing the terminal for Drush

The drush-cli command adds a few environment settings to our terminal session so we can issue Drush commands even faster. Among other things, it adds the following features after being executed:

- Execute all Drush commands against a specific site.
- Change directory to the root, modules, or files directories of a site.
- List files within a directory of a site.
- Execute commands without having to type drush at the start.

We will first enter on the Drush CLI and test a few commands. Then we will explain how to add Drush CLI configuration to our default terminal profile.

Starting a Drush CLI is as easy as executing the following command:

```
$ drush core-cli
Entering the drush cli.  Use CONTROL-D to exit.
Type 'help' for help.
drush>
```

Now we will load one of our site aliases and execute a few commands such as changing directory, listing files and clearing the cache:

```
drush> use @drupal.local
@drupal.local>
@drupal.local> cd %files
cd /home/juampy/projects/drupal/sites/default/files
@drupal.local> cd %root
cd /home/juampy/projects/drupal
@drupal.local> lsd %files
ls /home/juampy/projects/drupal/sites/default/files
styles
@drupal.local> cache-clear all
'all' cache was cleared  [success]
```

Note in the previous commands how the prompt changed to our site alias (**@drupal. local>**) to denote that the commands would be executed against that site. We can list files or change directory using simple placeholders such as %root or %files. Furthermore, we do not even need to type drush when executing commands such as cache-clear.

In the following example, we will remove the current site alias from the prompt and clear the cache of a remote site. Then we will use that remote site alias to see how the prompt formats remote site aliases and clear the cache again:

```
@drupal.local> use
drush>
drush> @drupal.dev cache-clear all
'all' cache was cleared   [success]
drush> use @festival.dev
festival.dev.drush:@festival.dev>
festival.dev.drush:@festival.dev> cache-clear all
'all' cache was cleared   [success]
```

Saving Drush CLI configuration into our profile

If you always want to open terminal sessions with Drush CLI loaded, you can configure your terminal profile by adding the --pipe option to drush-cli and append the output to your $HOME/.bashrc file. We will first make a backup of .bashrc to easily roll back. The following is how:

```
$ cd $HOME
$ cp .bashrc .bashrc.backup
$ drush core-cli --pipe >> .bashrc
$ source .bashrc
$ use @drupal.local
@drupal.local> status
 Drupal version        :  7.12
 Site URI              :  drupal.localhost
 Database driver       :  mysql
```

We first copied $HOME/.bashrc to .bashrc.backup and then added Drush CLI configuration to it. The source command used next reloads our terminal session, thus loading the new configuration. That is why we could use a site alias and execute the status command against it. Now if you open a new terminal you will already have this configuration set up. If you ever want to get back to a normal terminal by default, rename .bashrc.backup to .bashrc.

If you have **Shell scripting** skills, read the output generated by `drush core-cli --pipe` to see if you want to customize it further.

Summary

We have covered two aspects of Drush customization in this chapter: scripts (either commands or actual PHP scripts) and configuration for Drush or Drupal sites.

This chapter started with a step guide on how to write custom Drush commands and execute scripts against a bootstrapped Drupal site. Then, hooks for altering commands were presented as a great tool to perform extra tasks. Finally, the various ways to configure how Drush should behave system-wide or site-wide were explained with some examples: configuration files are short cuts to set command default options while site aliases give us the power to manage remote sites with short commands and synchronize sites easily.

Drush is highly configurable and once you get some practice using the contents covered in this chapter you will end up with a much more powerful Drush.

4
Extending Drush

This chapter will teach you to expand the Drush toolkit by installing and testing contributed modules. Each of them adds a set of commands for different purposes such as:

- Backing up and migrating entire sites to a wide range of destinations
- Reinstalling modules, inspecting source code, and generating test data
- Exporting configuration from database to a module
- Generating boilerplate code for custom modules
- Packaging a set of modules into a make file
- Managing and reverting views

Many contributed modules at `http://drupal.org` have a Drush extension which helps commands to perform some of their tasks. The previous examples are the most popular ones.

Backing up and migrating sites

The **Backup and Migrate** module manages backups elegantly. It has a great web interface to configure and execute backing up and restoring tasks. At its Drush extension there are a few shortcuts to accomplish tasks, such as:

- Generating and restoring a database backup of a site
- Listing existing backups and sources
- Getting a list of available destinations for backups, such as server or FTP directories, MySQL databases, Amazon S3 Bucket, or e-mail addresses
- Viewing the list of configured backup profiles

Installing the module and looking at the help information

Backup and Migrate is downloaded and installed like any other command that depends on a Drupal site. Here are the commands to achieve it:

```
$ cd /home/juampy/projects/drupal
$ drush pm-download backup_migrate
Project backup_migrate (7.x-2.2) downloaded to        [success]
  /home/juampy/projects/drupal/sites/all/modules/contrib/
  backup_migrate.

$ drush pm-enable --yes backup_migrate
The following extensions will be enabled: backup_migrate
Do you really want to continue? (y/n): y
backup_migrate was enabled successfully.              [ok]
```

The commands defined by Backup and Migrate are grouped within the output of drush `help`. This is because the module has implemented `hook_drush_help()`.

Here is the source code:

```
/**
 * Implementation of hook_drush_help().
 */
function backup_migrate_drush_help($section) {
  switch ($section) {
    case 'drush:bam-backup':
      return dt("Backup the site's database using default settings.");
    case 'drush:bam-restore':
      return dt('Restore the site\'s database with Backup and
Migrate.');
    case 'drush:bam-destinations':
      return dt('Get a list of available destinations.');
    case 'drush:bam-profiles':
      return dt('Get a list of available settings profiles.');
    case 'drush:bam-backups':
      return dt('Get a list of previously created backup files.');
  }
}
```

In the previous `hook`, each command description is used for the output of the `help` command. Here is how it gets formatted:

```
$ drush help --filter="backup_migrate"
All commands in backup_migrate: (backup_migrate)
 bam-backup (bb)        Backup the site's database with Backup and
                        Migrate.
 bam-backups            Get a list of previously created backup files.
 bam-destinations       Get a list of available destinations.
 bam-profiles           Get a list of available settings profiles.
 bam-restore            Restore the site's database with Backup and
                        Migrate.
 bam-sources            Get a list of available sources.
```

> Before you start using this module in Drupal 7, you must have defined and configured *right* permissions of the private files system path at **Admin | Configuration | File System**.

Generate and restore a backup

Now, we will test how the available commands work together. We will download and install the module, list the resources available, generate a backup on our testing Drupal site, and finally restore it:

1. List the available sources to backup. By default, there is only one which is our site database.

    ```
    $ drush bam-sources
     ID     Name                    Operations
     db     Default Database        configure, source
    ```

> The previous table is formatted using `drush_print_table()`, which receives the contents of the table and some extra parameters to structure output in columns.

2. List the available destinations to store backups. There are a few ones predefined by the module; but in this example, we will use the `manual` destination:

```
$ drush bam-destinations
ID              Name                        Operations

manual          Manual Backups Directory    manual backup,
                                              restore, list files,
                                              configure, delete

scheduled       Scheduled Backups           scheduled backup,
                Directory                     restore, list files,
                                              configure, delete

download        Download                    manual backup

upload          Upload                      restore

db              Default Database            configure, source
```

3. Now list the available backup profiles. A **profile** is a set of settings which define how you want the backup contents to be created.

```
$ drush bam-profiles
ID          Name

default     Default Settings
```

4. Generate a backup using default settings which are: our current database as the source, the `manual` backups directory as the destination, and the default profile:

```
$ drush bam-backup
Default Database backed up successfully to        [success]
Festival-2012-01-29T02-56-45 in destination Manual Backups
Directory in 652.4 ms.
```

5. The previous command saved our backup at `sites/default/files/ private/backup_migrate/manual/`.

6. Next, list the available backups in the `manual` destination, where our new backup file appears:

```
$ drush bam-backups manual
Filename                Date                    Age       Size

Festival-2012-01-       Sun, 01/29/2012 - 02:56  3 min     492.99KB
  29T02-56-45.mysql
```

7. Finally, restore our backup by giving its destination (our current database), the source (the `manual` backups directory), and the backup ID (the backup filename):

```
$ drush bam-restore db manual Festival-2012-01-29T02-56-45.mysql

Default Database restored from Manual Backups        [success]
Directory file Festival-2012-01-29T02-56-45.mysql in 24404.7 ms.
381 SQL commands executed.
```

As you can see, generating and restoring backups is a matter of using a couple of commands: `bam-backup` and `bam-restore`. The real work comes with configuring sources, destinations, and profiles in the web interface.

Reinstall, inspect modules, and generate data

The Drush extension of the **Devel** module provides a set of tools to speed up the development process of Drupal projects. This module's commands are for:

- Reinstalling enabled modules: disable, uninstall, and reinstall a module with just one command
- Search and inspect implementations of hooks and functions within all modules
- Generate users, nodes, taxonomies, and menus on the fly

Installing the module

Devel module is installed like any other module. We will take the chance to install `devel_generate` submodule too, as we will use it in the examples.

```
$ cd /home/juampy/projects/drupal

$ drush pm-download devel

Project devel (7.x-1.2) downloaded to /home/juampy/
projects/drupal/sites/all/modules/contrib/devel.
[success]

Project devel contains 3 modules: devel_generate, devel, devel_node_
access.
```

```
$ drush pm-enable --yes devel devel_generate

The following extensions will be enabled: devel, devel_generate

Do you really want to continue? (y/n): y

devel_generate was enabled successfully.              [ok]

devel was enabled successfully.              [ok]
```

FirePHP has been exported via svn to /home/juampy/projects/
drupal/sites/all/modules/contrib/devel/FirePHPCore.
[success]

Right after Devel module was enabled, the FirePHP was downloaded and installed within the module path. This was achieved by implementing the hook drush_ MODULE_post_COMMAND(). The following is its implementation extracted from the Drush command file within the module. It first checks if the Devel module was asked to be enabled and if so, calls another function to download FirePHP.

```
/**
 * Implements drush_MODULE_post_COMMAND().
 */
function drush_devel_post_pm_enable() {
  $extensions = func_get_args();
  // Deal with comma delimited extension list.
  if (strpos($extensions[0], ',') !== FALSE) {
    $extensions = explode(',', $extensions[0]);
  }

  if (in_array('devel', $extensions) && !drush_get_option('skip')) {
    drush_devel_download();
  }
}
```

Reinstalling modules

Sometimes we need to reinstall a module, for example, when you change the schema of a new module under development. This process involves three commands (pm-disable, pm-uninstall, and pm-enable). The Devel module implements a command to accomplish this: devel-reinstall. In the following example, we will download and install the Twitter module and then reinstall it again using this command:

```
$ cd /home/juampy/projects/drupal

$ drush pm-download twitter
```

```
Project twitter (7.x-3.0-beta4) downloaded to       [success]
/home/juampy/projects/drupal/sites/all/modules/contrib/twitter.
```

```
Project twitter contains 4 modules:
  twitter_signin, twitter_post, twitter_actions, twitter.


$ drush pm-enable --yes twitter
The following extensions will be enabled: twitter
Do you really want to continue? (y/n): y
twitter was enabled successfully.              [ok]


$ drush devel-reinstall  --yes twitter
The following extensions will be disabled: twitter
Do you really want to continue? (y/n): y
twitter was disabled successfully.          [ok]
The following modules will be uninstalled: twitter
Do you really want to continue? (y/n): y
twitter was successfully uninstalled.           [ok]
The following extensions will be enabled: twitter
Do you really want to continue? (y/n): y
twitter was enabled successfully.          [ok]
```

As we can see in the previous output, `devel-reinstall` calls the project management commands internally to disable, uninstall, and reinstall the module for us. Here is the command `callback` that creates an array with the three commands to execute and then calls `drush_invoke()` to run them:

```
/**
 * A command callback. This is faster than 3 separate bootstraps.
 */
function drush_devel_reinstall() {
  $projects = func_get_args();

  $args = array_merge(array('pm-disable'), $projects);
  call_user_func_array('drush_invoke', $args);

  $args = array_merge(array('pm-uninstall'), $projects);
  call_user_func_array('drush_invoke', $args);

  $args = array_merge(array('pm-enable'), $projects);
  call_user_func_array('drush_invoke', $args);
}
```

Inspecting source code

In Drupal sites, source code is spread among a long list of modules. This makes having precise tools, for finding hook implementations or functions, within a directory essential. Devel makes this process easier, by providing a command to search for implementations of a hook (fn-hook) or for any function or method (fn-view). We will now go through each of these two commands.

Searching for hook implementations

The fn-hook command has a simple syntax and interactive flow. By providing a hook name, a list of modules implementing it, is presented onscreen as a set of choices. Selecting one of these, prints the file name, the line number, and the source code. Here is an example where we look for implementations of hook_node_insert() and then choose the one in **Comment** module:

```
$ drush fn-hook node_insert
Enter the number of the hook implementation you wish to view.
  [0]  :  Cancel
  [1]  :  comment
  [2]  :  menu
  [3]  :  path
1
// file: /home/juampy/projects/drupal/modules/comment/comment.module,
lines 1288-1303
/**
 * Implements hook_node_insert().
 */
function comment_node_insert($node) {
  // Allow bulk updates and inserts to temporarily disable the
  // maintenance of the {node_comment_statistics} table.
  if (variable_get('comment_maintain_node_statistics', TRUE)) {
    db_insert('node_comment_statistics')
      ->fields(array(
        'nid' => $node->nid,
        'cid' => 0,
        'last_comment_timestamp' => $node->changed,
        'last_comment_name' => NULL,
```

```
        'last_comment_uid' => $node->uid,
        'comment_count' => 0,
    ))
    ->execute();
  }
}
```

As we can see, after selecting one of the choices, we get the full path to the file that contains the hook, and the start and end lines within that file. After that is the hook source code, which saves us from opening the file with a text editor.

> The choice list is formatted using drush_choice(), which receives the list of options, a text, and how each option is presented.

Viewing source code of functions and methods

If you know the name of the function or method that you are looking for, you can use fn-view to print its contents, and even open the file which contains it by passing its full path to a text editor.

In the following example, we print the source code of the function block_get_blocks_by_region(). Note that the full path, and start and end line numbers are printed at the top of the output:

```
$ drush fn-view block_get_blocks_by_region
// file: /home/juampy/projects/drupal/modules/block/block.module, lines
313-319
/**
 * Get a renderable array of a region containing all enabled blocks.
 *
 * @param $region
 *    The requested region.
 */
function block_get_blocks_by_region($region) {
  $build = array();
  if ($list = block_list($region)) {
    $build = _block_get_renderable_array($list);
  }
  return $build;
}
```

Now, we want to open the file (where the function is) with a text editor. In order to achieve this, we will use the option --pipe, which prints the filename instead of the source code. We will first test it and then wrap it with left ticks which will pipe the file path to our preferred editor (in this example, Vim):

```
$ drush fn-view --pipe block_get_blocks_by_region

/home/juampy/projects/drupal/modules/block/block.module

$ vim `drush fn-view --pipe block_get_blocks_by_region`
```

The previous command will launch our text editor and open the file. In the previous chapters, we have used the left ticks for piping the output of a command for another command (as we did with the sql-connect and sql-dump commands in *Chapter 2, Executing Drush Commands*).

Generating users and nodes

Devel can create users, nodes, taxonomies, and menus for us with a single command. This is a killer feature in the early stages of a project when we need some fake data to populate our site and to how it would look like when it gets real data.

Here are a few examples of how you can generate data of different kinds:

1. Create 20 nodes of type page with a maximum of 15 comments per node and delete all previous content by using the option --kill:

   ```
   $ drush generate-content --kill --types=page 20 15

   Finished creating 20 nodes                    [status]

   Generated 20 nodes, 15 comments (or less) per node.   [success]
   ```

2. Create 2 menus with 40 links, 5 levels of depth and 10 links maximum at the first level. Delete previously generated menus before starting:

   ```
   $ drush generate-menus --kill 2 40 5 10

   Generated 2 menus, 40 links.                  [success]

   Deleted existing menus and links.             [status]

   Created the following new menus:              [status]
   tiphite

   pradre

   Created 40 new menu links.                    [status]
   ```

3. Create a taxonomy vocabulary and add 50 terms to it:

   ```
   $ drush generate-vocabs 1

   Generated 1 vocabularies.                     [success]
   ```

```
Created the following new vocabularies: sipuwake      [status]
$ drush generate-terms sipuwake 50
Generated 50 terms.              [success]
Created the following new terms:              [status]
guuo
shimobobi
gulauetihuni
...
```

In the previous output we used two commands. The first one (generate-vocabs) created a vocabulary called sipuwake, which we used in the second command (generate-terms) to create 50 terms for it.

4. Create 20 users with role IDs 4 and 5, and delete all users before starting:

```
$ drush generate-users 20 --roles=4,5 --kill
Generated 20 users.          [success]
20 users deleted.            [status]
20 users created.            [status]
```

The commands used in the previous examples (generate-content, generate-menus, generate-vocabs, generate-terms, and generate-users) are more than enough to populate a site with testing data, saving us from clicking around the administration interface hundreds of times creating nodes, users, vocabularies, and terms. These commands try to populate as much data as possible, for example, if we create nodes from a content type that has images, it will create and upload them.

Working with features

The **Features** module is an outstanding solution for exporting module or site configuration that resides in the database as source code within a module. This has the following benefits:

- Features can store menus, user permissions, site settings, views, and contexts, among many others. Each of these is a **feature component**
- You can check which feature components have changed in the database by comparing them against the source code in the feature
- Features, as modules, can be installed in other sites, which helps reusability
- The source code of a feature can be version-controlled like any other module

You should have basic skills of using the Features module, through the administration interface, in order to make the most out of the following examples. A good place to start is at the documentation home page at http://drupal.org/node/580026.

In this example, we will create a view, add it to a feature, change the view, and see how the feature reflects this change. Here are the steps:

1. Go to **Structure** | **Views** | **Add new view**, create a simple view that lists nodes of type page with the title *Simple Node Listing*.

2. Download and install **Features** and **Diff** modules. The latter is used to view the differences between configuration in the database and in the feature.

    ```
    $ drush pm-download features diff

    Project features (7.x-1.0-beta6) downloaded to     [success]
        /home/juampy/projects/drupal/sites/all/modules/contrib/features.

    Project diff (7.x-2.0) downloaded to               [success]
        /home/juampy/projects/drupal/sites/all/modules/contrib/diff.


    $ drush pm-enable --yes features diff

    The following extensions will be enabled: features, diff

    Do you really want to continue? (y/n): ydiff was enabled
    successfully.                     [ok]

    features was enabled successfully.                 [ok]
    ```

The prompt asking for confirmation to continue is using drush_ confirm(), which receives the question to ask and returns TRUE or FALSE.

3. Create a feature to store the view you created in code. For this, we will make use of the features-export command, which accepts a feature name and a list of components to add to it. We will first list the available feature components to find the one with the name of our view:

    ```
    $ drush features-export

    ...

    views_view:frontpage

    views_view:glossary

    views_view:comments_recent

    views_view:simple_node_listing
    ```

```
views_view:taxonomy_term
views_view:tracker
dependencies:block
...
```

4. The feature component name of our view is `views_view:simple_node_listing`. Now, we can call the `features-export` command to create a feature called `feature_node_listing`:

```
$ drush features-export feature_node_listing
  views_view:simple_node_listing
```

```
Created module: feature_node_listing in          [ok]
  sites/all/modules/feature_node_listing
```

5. If you open the source code of any of the files at `sites/all/modules/feature_node_listing`, you will see that it holds all the settings of the view `Simple Node Listing`. This will be used later on to track changes on its configuration.

6. Now if we list all features with `feature-list` command, we will see our feature:

```
$ drush features-list
```

Name	Feature	Status	State
feature_node_listing	*feature_node_listing*	*Disabled*	
Features Tests	features_test	Disabled	

> Keep in mind that features are modules whose code is generated automatically by **Features**. As such, they can be treated like any other module through the project management commands such as `pm-enable`, `pm-list`, and others.

7. Our feature is listed, but its status is `Disabled`. We will enable it like we would do for a normal module so we can track its `State`:

```
$ drush pm-enable feature_node_listing
The following extensions will be enabled: feature_node_listing
Do you really want to continue? (y/n): y
feature_node_listing was enabled successfully.          [ok]
$ drush features-list
```

Name	Feature	Status	State
feature_node_listing	*feature_node_listing*	*Enabled*	
Features Tests	features_test	Disabled	

8. Now, let's change something at the `Simple Node Listing` view to see how the `State` changes. Go to **Structure | Views | Edit Simple Node Listing view** and change the page display name to **Node Listing**. Save your changes and then in the command line list all features again as in the following example:

```
$ drush features-list
```

Name	Feature	Status	State
feature_node_listing	feature_node_listing	Enabled	Overridden
Features Tests	features_test	Disabled	

9. Our feature shows an `Overridden` state. This means that the configuration in the database does not match with the one in the feature code. As we have installed the Diff module, Features can print a list of differences with the `features-diff` command. the following are the current differences between the `Simple Node Listing` view in the database and the one in our feature:

```
$ drush features-diff feature_node_listing

Legend:

Code:        drush features-revert will remove the overrides.

Overrides:   drush features-update will update the exported feature
with the displayed overrides

Component: views_view

);

<    /* Display: Page */

<    $handler = $view->new_display('page', 'Page', 'page');

---

>    /* Display: Node listing */

>    $handler = $view->new_display('page', 'Node listing', 'page');

    $handler->display->display_options['path'] = 'simple-node-
listing';

      '

    )
```

10. The previous output prints the differences using the syntax of the `diff` command from Linux. We can clearly see in the highlighted lines that, currently, the title of the page display is `Node listing` in the database, while in the feature module it is `Page`.

In order to format the differences with colors, Features
checks if the terminal supports them by checking the
value of one of Drush's environment variables through
`drush_get_context('DRUSH_NOCOLOR')`.

11. When a feature is in an `Overridden` state, we can either revert it or update it.
    Reverting a feature means to push what is in the source code to the database
    (thus, setting the title back to `Page`), while updating a feature means pulling
    what is in the database into source code (hence keeping the page title to `Node
    Listing`). Both actions will set the feature back to a default state. Here is how
    we could update it using `features-update`:

```
$ drush features-update --yes feature_node_listing

Module appears to already exist in
  sites/all/modules/feature_node_listing

Do you really want to continue? (y/n): y

Created module: feature_node_listing in           [ok]
  sites/all/modules/feature_node_listing
```

12. Alternatively, the `features-revert` undoes the changes we did on the view:

```
$ drush features-revert --yes feature_node_listing

Do you really want to revert views_view? (y/n): y

Reverted views_view.          [ok]
```

13. Reverting or updating a feature, changes its status to default. If we list
    features again, we will not see the `Overridden` status:

```
$ drush features-list
```

Name	Feature	Status	State
feature_node_listing	feature_node_listing	Enabled	
Features Tests	features_test	Disabled	

The `State` column is blank now, which means that our feature is again in a
default state. This means that its configuration in code matches with the one
in the database.

Once a feature module has been created, we can still add more components to it. Imagine, that we want to add the permission to administer views to our existing feature. We will first list the available feature components by giving the feature name to the `features-add` command and then add it:

```
$ drush features-add feature_node_listing
 Available components

 ...

 user_permission:change own username

 user_permission:cancel account

 user_permission:select account cancellation method

 user_permission:administer views

 user_permission:access all views

 views_view:archive

 views_view:backlinks

 ...

$ drush features-add feature_node_listing
  "user_permission:administer views"
Module appears to already exist in
  sites/all/modules/feature_node_listing
Do you really want to continue? (y/n): y
Created module: feature_node_listing in          [ok]
  sites/all/modules/feature_node_listing
```

The previous command added the permission to administer views to our feature. Note that, as the feature component name has spaces, we wrapped it with quotes so Drush will not take it as two different feature components. If you view the source code of `sites/all/modules/feature_node_listing`, you will see that it holds both (the view and the permission).

The Features module is normally used to propagate configuration and data to other Drupal instances and to highlight when a component has changed. Module configuration can be added to a feature by installing the **Strongarm** module (`http://drupal.org/project/strongarm`) and a fine-grain level of component picking can be achieved with the **Features Plumber** module (`http://drupal.org/project/features_plumber`). There are many other modules which support or extend Features which can be found at `http://drupal.org/project/modules` by searching the **Features Package** category.

Managing views from the command line

The **Views** module adds a set of commands to perform actions such as:

- Listing details and status of the existing views in a site
- Disabling or enabling a view
- Setting up Views module configuration to debug views easily
- Reverting a view to its default state

We will go over a few examples using the view and feature that we created in the previous section.

The command `views-list` gives us an overview of all the installed views, the status of each one, and some statistics at the bottom. Here is the output when being executed at our testing Drupal site:

```
$ cd /home/juampy/projects/drupal
$ drush views-list
 Machine name            Description     Type      Status     Tag
 simple_node_listing                     Default   Enabled    default
 tweets                  Displays...     Default   Enabled
 ...
A total of 9 views were found in this Drupal installation:
  0 views reside only in the database
  0 views are overridden
  9 views are in their default state
  7 views are disabled
```

We can see in the previous output, that our custom view `simple_node_listing` is listed among other views. Now, we will enable some settings in the Views module with the command `views-dev`, which will help us when we edit views in development environments. This command sets up a few Views configuration variables to provide extended information about the installed views. We can activate it with the following command:

```
$ drush views-dev
Setup the new views settings.          [success]
```

The previous command helps us when editing a view in the administration interface by doing things such as automatically expanding the **Advanced** tab, showing the master display, previewing results, showing the generated SQL query, and printing performance statistics, among others.

The views in a Drupal site can also be disabled and enabled through the command line, thanks to the commands `views-disable` and `views-enable` respectively. Here is an example where we disable and then enable our custom view:

```
$ drush views-disable simple_node_listing
The view 'simple_node_listing' has been disabled        [success]
Views cache was cleared             [ok]
Menu cache was cleared              [ok]


$ drush views-enable simple_node_listing
The view 'simple_node_listing' has been enabled        [success]
Views cache was cleared                 [ok]
Menu cache was cleared                  [ok]
```

The status of a view can be tracked if it has been added to a feature. In the previous section, we created a feature called `feature_node_listing` and a custom view (`simple_node_listing`) of it. With this set up, Drupal can compare the settings of the view stored in the database against the ones defined by the feature and tell us whether the view has been changed or not. Let's demonstrate this with an example. Using the administration interface, open **Admin | Structure | Views | Edit the view Simple Node Listing** by changing anything on it and then save your changes. Then, open the terminal to list the existing views with the `views-list` command:

```
$ drush views-list
  Machine name            Description        Type         Status        Tag
  simple_node_listing                        Overridden   Enabled       default

...

A total of 9 views were found in this Drupal installation:
  0 views reside only in the database
  1 views are overridden
  8 views are in their default state
  7 views are disabled
```

Our view `simple_node_listing` shows an `Overridden` status. We can revert this view to its default status by using the `views-revert` command:

```
$ drush views-revert simple_node_listing
Reverted the view 'simple_node_listing'        [success]
Reverted a total of 1 views.        [ok]
```

Now if we list views again, we will see that our view has the status default back.

```
$ drush views-list
  Machine name          Description    Type         Status       Tag
   simple_node_listing                 Default      Enabled      default
...
A total of 9 views were found in this Drupal installation:
   0 views reside only in the database
   0 views are overridden
   9 views are in their default state
   7 views are disabled
```

The Drush commands, provided by the Views module, help us track the status of each view and enable a few settings to work with them with extended information. We can also see similarities between views-revert and features-revert commands, the former being a subset of the latter.

Generating a custom module codebase

During a project, it is very likely that we will have to create one or more custom modules. This, at the very least, involves creating a directory at sites/all/modules/custom/module_name, plus the module_name.info and module_name.module files within that directory with some hook implementations. **Module Builder** provides a very powerful Drush command to generate all the boilerplate code that we need to start working with our module.

 Unfortunately there is no Windows support for Module Builder.

We will create a module that implements the hooks hook_menu(), hook_block(), hook_theme(), and hook_permission(). The command mb-build launches an interactive process to gather all the information needed to create the module. Here is an example, where we download and install it and then create our custom module:

```
$ drush pm-download module_builder

Project module_builder (7.x-2.x-dev) downloaded to         [success]
  /home/juampy/projects/drupal/sites/all/modules/contrib/module_builder.


$ drush pm-enable --yes module_builder
```

```
The following extensions will be enabled: module_builder
Do you really want to continue? (y/n): y
module_builder was enabled successfully.                [ok]


$drush mb-build --write
Enter the module name: sample_module
Enter the required hook presets:
Enter the required hooks: menu permission theme block
Enter the human readable name: Sample Module
Enter the description: Just a sample module
Enter the help text: This module serves as a simple example of
        module code generation
Enter the dependencies:
Enter the package:


Proposed sample_module.module:
<?php
/**
 * @file sample_module.module
 * TODO: Enter file description here.
 */


/**
 * Implements hook_help().
 */
function sample_module_help($path, $arg) {
  switch ($path) {
    case 'admin/help#sample_module':
...
$ ls sites/all/modules/sample_module
sample_module.info   sample_module.module
```

The previous command, after entering the required information, created the module directory structure for us (the `--write` option is needed for this) and printed the contents of each file onscreen. Now, if we check out the contents of `sites/all/modules/sample_module/sample_module.module`, we will see that it has added a very clean and descriptive syntax for each of the hooks that we specified, including suggestions of what our next steps could be.

Packaging module information in make files

Drush Make packages module information so you can build a Drupal installation with a set of downloaded modules. By turning the `make` file into an installation profile, you can go one step further by enabling modules and preconfiguring the Drupal site, which leads to ready to use Drupal distributions such as **Open Atrium** (`http://openatrium.com`), **Open Public** (`http://drupal.org/project/openpublic`), or **Commons** (`http://drupal.org/project/commons`).

Now we will create our own Drupal distribution. Let's suppose that we have been working on a site for promoting our favorite music festival. There is stuff in this site that we would like to use in future festival websites. We will first install Drush Make and then generate a `make` file out of our existing site.

Installing Drush Make

If you are using Drush 5 or installed Drush in Windows through the installer, you can skip this step because Drush 5 incorporates Drush Make.

Drush Make has commands that do not depend on a Drupal site, such as the `make` command, which, given a `make` file, downloads and creates a Drupal installation. For this reason, instead of downloading it as a normal module we are going to place it at our `.drush` directory so it will be available from anywhere in the command line. Drush does this for us automatically by executing the `pm-download` command from a non-Drupal directory.

```
$ cd $HOME
$ drush dl drush_make-6.x
Project drush_make (6.x-2.3) downloaded to /home/juampy/.drush/drush_
make.          [success]
Project drush_make contains 0 modules: .
```

Drush Make works for both Drupal 6 and 7 versions. That is why we specified version 6.x (there is no 7.x branch for this project). Now, let's test that the Drush Make commands are available:

```
$ drush help | grep make
Other commands: (drush_make,drush_make_d_o)
  convert-makefile          Convert the specified makefile to a
                            drupal.org friendly format, and verify the
                            converted file.
```

make	*Turns a makefile into a working drupal install.*
make-generate *(generate-makefile)*	*Attempts to generate a makefile from the current Drupal install, specifying project version numbers unless not known or otherwise specified. Unversioned projects will be interpreted later by drush make as "most recent stable release"*
make-test	Run a drush make test.
verify-makefile	Verify the specified makefile is in a drupal.org friendly format.

As we can see in the help information, the Drush Make commands are discovered by Drush. Now we will generate our make file.

Generating a make file out of an existing site

In the following example, we will use the two highlighted commands (make-generate and make) to create a make file with all the module information about our existing Drupal site.

Gathering information about our site and writing a make file

Generate a festival.make file by placing ourselves at the root of our site and executing the make-generate command:

```
$ cd /home/juampy/projects/festival
$ drush make-generate festival.make
Project information for ctools retrieved.              [ok]
Project information for features retrieved.            [ok]
Project information for twitter retrieved.             [ok]
Project information for views retrieved.               [ok]
Some of the properties in your makefile will have to be  [error]
manually edited. Please do that now.
Wrote .make file festival.make                         [ok]
```

The previous command raised a warning because some of our modules do not have a version number because either they are development releases such as, the Devel module, or they simply do not exist at http://drupal.org such as, the feature that we created in the Features section of this chapter.

In order to fix this, we will simply edit the generated `festival.make` file and remove all the information related to modules which are not in a stable state or are custom. We will also set the subdirectory path of each module to be `contrib` so when we are building a Drupal installation with this `make` file, the modules listed in it will be downloaded at `sites/all/modules/contrib`. Here is how the file `festival.make` would look after our edits:

```
; This file was auto-generated by drush_make
core = 7.x
api = 2
projects[drupal][version] = "7.10"

; Modules
projects[ctools][subdir] = "contrib"
projects[ctools][version] = "1.0-rc1"
projects[features][subdir] = "contrib"
projects[features][version] = "1.0-beta6"
projects[twitter][subdir] = "contrib"
projects[twitter][version] = "3.0-beta4"
projects[views][subdir] = "contrib"
projects[views][version] = "3.1"

; Modules
; Please fill the following out. Type may be one of get, cvs, git, bzr
or svn,
; and url is the url of the download.
projects[devel][download][type] = ""
projects[devel][download][url] = ""
projects[devel][type] = "module"
…
```

As you can see in the contents of `festival.make`, it defines a version of Drupal core that it will download, and a set of modules with their version numbers and destination paths. You can edit this file freely and add more modules to it.

> The `README.txt` file of the Drush Make module provides extended information of how to download modules from Git repositories, apply patches, and download themes or libraries among other tasks.

Loading contents from the make file into a Drupal installation

Now, move festival.make out of the current Drupal installation and invoke the make command to create a new Drupal installation out of festival.make.

```
$ mv festival.make ../
$ cd ..
$ drush make festival.make other_festival
Project information for drupal retrieved          [ok]
Project information for ctools retrieved.          [ok]
Project information for features retrieved.        [ok]
Project information for twitter retrieved.         [ok]
Project information for views retrieved.           [ok]
drupal downloaded from                             [ok]
  http://ftp.drupal.org/files/projects/drupal-7.10.tar.gz.
ctools downloaded from                             [ok]
  http://ftp.drupal.org/files/projects/ctools-7.x-1.0-rc1.tar.gz.
features downloaded from                           [ok]
  http://ftp.drupal.org/files/projects/features-7.x-1.0-beta6.tar.gz.
twitter downloaded from                            [ok]
  http://ftp.drupal.org/files/projects/twitter-7.x-3.0-beta4.tar.gz.
views downloaded from                              [ok]
  http://ftp.drupal.org/files/projects/views-7.x-3.1.tar.gz.
```

This command has created a new directory called other_festival and downloaded Drupal 7.10 and the list of modules defined at festival.make. Here are the contents of the sites/all/modules/contrib directory:

```
$ cd other_festival
$ ls sites/all/modules/contrib/
ctools  features  twitter  views
```

The modules defined at festival.make were downloaded to the directory we defined and have the version number given. Now, we can install a site within this Drupal installation and enable it.

You can find further information about building installation profiles out of make files at http://drupal.org/node/1006620. Also, http://drushmake.me has a very friendly web interface to create make files on the fly.

Summary

There is a long list of modules that incorporate a Drush extension. A full list can be found at http://drupal.org/project/modules?filters=tid%3A4654&solrsort=sis_project_release_usage%20desc. We have tested the most common ones and installed them in our Drupal site or in our .drush directory, depending on their nature. While testing their commands, we took the opportunity to explore features of the Drush API used by them.

You are encouraged to spend some time checking out the module list from the previous link. See if you can find more helpful modules.

Index

Thank you for buying
Drush User's Guide

About Packt Publishing

Packt, pronounced 'packed', published its first book "*Mastering phpMyAdmin for Effective MySQL Management*" in April 2004 and subsequently continued to specialize in publishing highly focused books on specific technologies and solutions.

Our books and publications share the experiences of your fellow IT professionals in adapting and customizing today's systems, applications, and frameworks. Our solution based books give you the knowledge and power to customize the software and technologies you're using to get the job done. Packt books are more specific and less general than the IT books you have seen in the past. Our unique business model allows us to bring you more focused information, giving you more of what you need to know, and less of what you don't.

Packt is a modern, yet unique publishing company, which focuses on producing quality, cutting-edge books for communities of developers, administrators, and newbies alike. For more information, please visit our website: www.packtpub.com.

About Packt Open Source

In 2010, Packt launched two new brands, Packt Open Source and Packt Enterprise, in order to continue its focus on specialization. This book is part of the Packt Open Source brand, home to books published on software built around Open Source licences, and offering information to anybody from advanced developers to budding web designers. The Open Source brand also runs Packt's Open Source Royalty Scheme, by which Packt gives a royalty to each Open Source project about whose software a book is sold.

Writing for Packt

We welcome all inquiries from people who are interested in authoring. Book proposals should be sent to author@packtpub.com. If your book idea is still at an early stage and you would like to discuss it first before writing a formal book proposal, contact us; one of our commissioning editors will get in touch with you.

We're not just looking for published authors; if you have strong technical skills but no writing experience, our experienced editors can help you develop a writing career, or simply get some additional reward for your expertise.

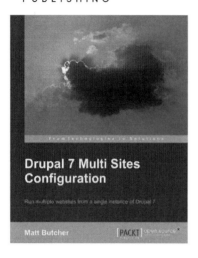

Drupal 7 Multi Sites Configuration

ISBN: 978-1-84951-800-0   Paperback: 100 pages

Run multiple website from a single instance of Drupal 7

1. Prepare your server for hosting multiple sites

2. Configure and install several sites on one instance of Drupal

3. Manage and share themes and modules across the multi-site configuration

Drupal E-commerce with Ubercart 2.x

ISBN: 978-1-847199-20-1   Paperback: 364 pages

Build administer, and customize an online store using Drupal with Ubercart

1. Create a powerful e-shop using the award-winning CMS Drupal and the robust e-commerce module Ubercart

2. Create and manage the product catalog and insert products in manual or batch mode

3. Apply SEO (search engine optimization) to your e-shop and adopt turn-key internet marketing techniques

4. Implement advanced techniques like cross-selling, product comparison, coupon codes, and segmented pricing

Please check **www.PacktPub.com** for information on our titles

Drupal 7 Themes

ISBN: 978-1-84951-276-3   Paperback: 320 pages

Create new themes for your Drupal 7 site with a clean
layout and powerful CSS styling

1. Learn to create new Drupal 7 themes

2. No experience of Drupal theming required

3. Discover techniques and tools for creating and
    modifying themes

4. The first book to guide you through the new
    elements and themes available in Drupal 7

Drupal 7 Development by
Example Beginner's Guide

ISBN: 978-1-84951-680-8   Paperback: 270 pages

Folow the creation of a Drupal website to learn, by
example, the key concepts of Drupal 7 development,
and HTML5

1. A hands-on, example-driven guide to
    programming Drupal websites

2. Discover a number of new features for Drupal
    7 through practical and interesting examples
    while building a fully functional recipe sharing
    website

3. Learn about web content management, multi-
    media integration, and e-commerce in Drupal 7

Please check **www.PacktPub.com** for information on our titles

Made in the USA
San Bernardino, CA
26 April 2013